# Rothamsted, Lawes and Dinosaurs

Bernard O'Connor

The Rothamsted Experimental Station outside Harpenden, in Hertfordshire, UK. is acknowledged as the world's first centre of agricultural research. It was established in 1843 by John Bennet Lawes, the owner of Rothamsted Manor, when he was only 29 years old. Lawes has been acknowledged in books on agricultural history as a major contributor to scientific farming, a contribution financed from the fortune he made from a company he set up to make superphosphate, one of the most popular fertilisers of the 19$^{th}$ century. This work will investigate the origins and development of the manure business, in particular the contribution paid by his involvement in a little acknowledged branch of agricultural mining - that of "coprolites."

Born in Rothamsted in 1814 he had unhappy years at Eton, but he did develop an interest in chemistry. According to an article in 'Modern London' he

> *"At the age of twenty, equipped one of the best bedrooms in the house with every requisite of a well appointed laboratory, and entered seriously into what he saw then to be the work of his life."*

(Modern London, 1888)

His studies at Brasenose College, Oxford, under Professor Daubeny, a chemist, botanist and geologist, made him aware of the developments being made in "High Farming". The introduction of these ideas since the mid-1700s was having an enormous impact on Great Britain's agriculture. Yields of cereals, vegetables, wool, meat and milk were increasing - as were farmers' profits. The doubling of the country's population in the first half of the 19$^{th}$ century dramatically stimulated demand for food, especially from the growing urban centres. Able-bodied and more motivated men and women flooded from the countryside to towns and cities to find work. Many of the poorer amongst them had been forced off the land by the introduction of the Enclosure Acts. Renting or buying accommodation in the typical two-up-two down terraced houses, they did not have a garden. Unable to grow their own vegetable, pick their own fruit or keep chickens or a pig, they needed to buy food from the nearest market or shop. Agriculturalists were keen to capitalise on this increased demand and experimented with a variety of methods to increase production.

Lawes had learned that a major contributor to plant growth was the soil's fertility. In attempts to increase this fertility farmers were experimenting with blood, soot, rags, fish, seaweed and ground and burnt animal bones. Even leftover bone and ivory dust from Sheffield cutlers was sold in 1836 at £4 a ton. Only producing 600 tons a year it could not meet the local farmers' demand. (Johnson, C.W. (1836), 'The Use of Crushed Bones as Manure', London) After boiling animal carcasses the bones were crushed or burnt and bagged up. Spread on fields they led to considerable success in increasing yields. Analytical chemists showed that the fertilising principle was their phosphate content. So great was farmers' demand for bone phosphate that manure manufacturers began purchasing huge quantities from the continent and North Africa where Great Britain had an imperial foothold. The analytical chemist, Professor Justus Von Liebig, commented that

> *"Great Britain was like a ghoul, searching the continents for bones to feed its agriculture... robbing all other countries of the condition of their fertility."*

("In Keatley, W.S. (1976), '100 years of Fertiliser Manufacture', Fertiliser Manufacturers Association (FMA))

He accused manure manufacturers of using bones from the battlefields of Leipzig, Waterloo and the Crimea. Even Sicilian catacombs were raided for their manure content and cargoes of mummified cats from Egyptian catacombs found their way into the manure manufacturers' dens. When Lawes went into business he likely continued these purchases. By 1839 the bone business was worth £150,000 per annum and about 30,000 tons were being imported annually. The Gardeners' Chronicle and Agricultural Gazette gave detailed accounts of the efficacy of these new manures. Lawes experimented with them on his Rothamsted estate himself. (Graham, J. (1839), 'A Treatise on the Use and Value of Manure', London p.6) However, he recognised that, apart from the problem of supply, crushed bones were insoluble. It also took a long time before their mineral potential in the soil water could be absorbed by the plant roots. Bones were also expensive and the machinery for grinding them had not been perfected. (Ibid.)

Once the chemists acknowledged that plant's major nutrient was phosphate the search was on to discover alternative supplies. In 1828 a rock phosphate, called phosphorite, had started being exploited in Ontario, Canada. Chemists had found its value as a fertiliser and samples were tested in Great Britain. The German explorer, Humboldt's mapping of the South American coastline led to the European's "discovering" the use of "huano" or guano - phosphate-rich bird droppings from the Peruvian islands of Chincha. It was imported into Liverpool from 1838 selling at up to £12 per ton. This was much more expensive that bones but a successful advertising campaign in the agricultural press led to its widespread usage.

## LAWES' EARLY EXPERIMENTS

Lawes experimented with guano and got better results than using crushed or burnt bones. However, with guano being very expensive, he was keen to develop cheaper manures. In 1839 he began experimenting to see what effect sulphuric acid had on burnt animal bones and mineral phosphates.

There is controversy over who first successfully used sulphuric acid in this way. Sir James Murray, MD., had successfully dissolved bones in Dublin as early as 1817 but did not patent it. Professor Liebig suggested it in his Agricultural Chemistry published in 1840. There is the possibility that one of Liebig's students, Joseph Henry Gilbert, who was later to join Lawes, may have mentioned it to him. He bought carboys of vitriol - huge glass containers of sulphuric acid - and a millstone to grind the phosphate materials.

The acid, bones and other phosphates were mixed in a huge iron trough in Lawes' barn. The resulting mixture was stirred until it set sufficiently to be taken out and heaped. During his experiments the barn door was kept ajar, not only to let the fumes escape but also so that his men could run outside and wash themselves in the nearby pond if they got splashed. He called the resultant mixture "Super Phosphate of Lime". He tested it by adding varying quantities to watering cans and used it on the various plants in pots and beds. His tests confirmed that it was soluble.

This was a major breakthrough in scientific farming. Whilst there is dispute over who was the first to discover this new fertiliser, Lawes knew he had a potential market winner and not just in Great Britain. He found that root crops, particularly turnips, had a significant increase in yield. Aware of the links between science and agriculture he wanted to take advantage of this discovery but, being a "gentleman", his mother discouraged him from engaging in trade, least of all in manures. The financial advantages, however, were too great to be ignored and in the same year he established Lawes Chemical Manure Company. (Russell, Sir E.J. (1942), 'British Agricultural Research: Rothamsted', pp.2-7)

He repeated his experiments using a wide range of phosphatic materials on a larger scale during 1840 - 41 with great success. He realised that a fortune could be made if he could start production of his "Super Phosphate of Lime" on a large scale. Production costs were low and superphosphate proved just as effective a fertiliser as guano. As it could be marketed at half the price he knew he could capture a large proportion of the expanding manure market. Accordingly, on the 23rd May 1842, he was granted a patent for certain improvements of Manures: -

> *"1 - By means of sulphuric acid, decomposing "bones, bone ash, bone dust, apatite, or phosphorite, and other phosphoritic substances" for purposes of manure.*
>
> *2. - Combining for manurial purposes phosphoric acid with any particular alkali, as potash or soda or magnesia or ammonia, or any earth containing such alkalis.*
>
> *3. - Making a manure by combining silica (in the state of ground flint or sand) with either potash or soda, or applying as manure crystal or glass ground to powder."*
>
> (Rothamsted Library Archives, A2)

It was hardly a coincidence but on exactly the same day, Sir James Murray took out a similar patent for the improvement of manures in Scotland. Lawes' patent was only valid up to Berwick upon Tweed. Adding to the confusion is the fact that a Scot, William Hay of Tillydesk, Ellon, according to his monument in the churchyard of St. Nicholas in Aberdeen, "*introduced and gave name to the manure called superphosphate in 1842*". Who then was actually the first to discover superphosphate is uncertain. Murray wanted to capitalise on his "discovery" and managed to publish his "Advice to Farmers" that year. (Murray, J. (1842), 'Advice to

Farmers,' Longman and Co.; Dyke, G.V. (1993), 'John Lawes of Rothamsted', Hoos press Harpenden, p.14) Lawes first advert in the Gardeners Chronicle for 1st July 1843 recommended his Superphosphate of lime "*for fixing the Ammonia of Dung-heaps, Cesspools and Gas Liquor*". It also revealed he was marketing Phosphate of Ammonia and Silicate of Potash at four shillings and sixpence (£0.22) per bushel.

To protect his patent Lawes successfully took legal action against Murray to disclaim the "*parts of the said specification which describe and claim the making of manure from Bone ash by decomposing the same by sulphuric acid.*" He stressed the importance of phosphoritic substances in his patent and felt that bone dust was "*tardy and imperfect*" and, unlike his Super Phosphate of Lime, of no use on turnips. (Ibid.)

Walter Palmer did the first trials of Lawes' turnip manure in 1842 on his farm in Swaffham, Cambs. He found it "*superior to farmyard manure,*" actually doubling his turnip yield. (Ibid.) Lawes must have been aware that his manure would increase the supply of winter fodder for cattle farmers. Most cattle were traditionally slaughtered before Christmas because of the shortage of fodder so any means of increasing turnip yields would allow cattle farmers to fatten their animals for longer. This would increase meat yields which in turn would command higher prices over Christmas and spring as well as increasing demand for his "super".

When Lawes got married he went back on a promise to his wife, Caroline, of a Grand Tour of Europe as a honeymoon. Instead they had a trip on the Thames during which he found a good site for his factory. He bought land at Deptford Creek, near Greenwich, and had a chemical factory erected to manufacture his superphosphate and associated products. (Communication with George Dyke, Rothamsted; Gray, A.N. (1930), ' Phosphates and Superphosphates', ISMA)

On June 1st, 1843, he engaged Joseph Gilbert as his full-time scientific collaborator and provided him with a residence in Harpenden. That was the day that Rothamsted Experimental Station was founded. Between them they applied for the first time on a large scale, scientific methods of testing a wide variety of manures and artificial fertilisers on different crops on the clayey soils of the estate. Over the years they achieved the well-documented results that made Rothamsted famous. They set down the scientific basis of rotation, studied the exact effects of various feeds on animals, and initiated investigations into botany, chemistry, meteorology as well as plant and animal physiology. (Stevenson, J.H. (1989), 'Rothamsted: a cradle of agricultural research', Plants Today, May-June, pp.84-89) It was Lawes financial ventures that funded much of the research at Rothamsted.

The same year, Liebig received a letter of introduction in which Lawes was described as "*a gentleman of fortune who has devoted himself for some years past to the elucidation of Agricultural Chemistry with great zeal and ability*." (Lawes Chemical Manure Company documents, Rural History Centre, Reading University) Liebig must have been aggrieved at Lawes' fortune. He intended to do the same. In October 1845 he took out his own patent to manufacture manures from Carbonate of Potash and Carbonate of Soda with Carbonate and Phosphate of Lime. There was an ongoing disagreement between him and Lawes that involved costly litigation. It was over Lawes' claim to use sulphuric acid. An important factor was that Lawes claimed five shillings (£0.25) royalty on every ton of superphosphate made by his competitors. (Dyke, G.V. op.cit.p.15)

## THE FIRST USE OF COPROLITES

During these legal proceedings Lawes was informed of a discovery which has been given little acknowledgement in the existing accounts of Lawes' financial success. Charles Darwin's Cambridge professor of Botany, Rev. John Henslow, had been given a living in Hitcham, Suffolk, and on a holiday to the Victorian watering hole of Felixstow in 1842. Whilst there, he discovered some fossils in the red crag of the cliffs. He took them to be "coprolites", the fossilised droppings of prehistoric creatures that lived on the edges of the shallow sea that surrounded what geologists term the 'London-Brabant Platform'. This covered much of Southern England about 120 - 90 million years ago.

In 1828 the Dean of Westminster, Rev. William Buckland had found coprolites of ichthyosaurus in the cliffs of Lyme Regis, Dorset. He shocked religious circles by showing that pre -Adamite creatures were cannibalistic. Bones of young ichthyosaurus were found in the contents of its stomach and intestines. He had earrings made from their polished sections - and a family table inlaid with them to amuse his visitors! (Brook, A.J. (1993), 'Rev. William Buckland, the first palaeoecologist' Biologist, p.152)

The fossils Henslow found had been used for generations as road filling material. An alternative use had been discovered in the 18$^{th}$ century when a cartload had overturned and the farmer noted that his turnip crop grew with "exceptional liveliness". The resultant yield was found to be significantly higher than the surrounding crop and farmers were soon using them as manure. (White, (1850), 'History of Suffolk') Henslow reckoned that these coprolites and fossil bone bed ought to be of commercial interest to the nation's manure manufacturers.

According to Rev. Buckland it was Liebig who "*...invited the attention of agriculturalists to the possibility of applying to* *the same use as bone dust and guano the fossil bones and coprolites*." (Buckland, W. (1849), 'On the Causes of the General Presence of Phosphates in the Strata of the Earth, and in all fertile soils; with Observations on Pseudo-coprolites." Journal of the Royal Agricultural Society, Vol.10, p.520) In the belief that the Felixstow deposit was coprolitic Henslow sent samples for analysis to the Cambridge geologist, Professor Solly, and the Cambridge chemist, Mr Isiah Deck. When their phosphatic content was confirmed he published several papers on the subject in agricultural and geological journals. Lawes most likely read them. When Henslow read a paper to the British Association for the Advancement of Science in Cambridge in 1845 on their agricultural value, Lawes took up the idea of dissolving "coprolites" in acid. He bought two tons of these Felixstow "coprolites" and had them tested. His analysis showed them to contain 53.5% phosphate of lime. In his correspondence with Henslow, he pointed out that,

> *"I have taken some trouble to procure a sufficient quantity to be tried this year as Superphosphate of lime in comparison with my own which is made from calcined bones but the owners have an exaggerated notion of their value that I have given up taken any further steps about it. I was told the other day that they were worth £14 per ton. The superphosphate that I make contains 50 parts of phosphate of lime and 30 parts Sulphuric acid in 100 and I sell this for £7 per ton. - Therefore I do not consider Coprolites to be worth a high price and the Carbonate of Lime would consume much acid to no purpose."*

(Rothamsted Archives, Correspondence, 13th June 1845)

According to Henslow, Lawes *then "abandoned the idea of their being a source to which he could have recourse, in consequence of the absurd notions which have got abroad of the extreme value of these nodules.*" (Henslow, J.S. (1848), Agricultural Gazette, p.520) However, other manure manufacturers in the area, William Colchester and Edward Packard of Ipswich and Joseph Fison of Thetford, had the "coprolites" ground in their mills and successfully dissolved them in sulphuric acid. They began marketing superphosphate but how many of them paid Lawes his royalties is unknown.

Their success in using "coprolites" as a raw material in their manure factories led Lawes to change his mind. By 1847 he too made arrangements for these "coprolites" to be shipped up the Thames to his Deptford factory. Here 120 - 150 ton ships carrying Peruvian guano, Chilean nitrate of soda and animal bones, hoofs, shoddy, dried blood from the continent were unloaded alongside Suffolk coprolites at the Canal Docks. (Gray, op.cit. p.10) He thus helped lay the foundations of what became a very important industry and became a pioneer in the very lucrative trade in both manure and "coprolites."

As a result, during the late 1840s, many parishes along the southeast Suffolk coast experienced a new industry, an alternative to the traditional farming and fishing work. Small scale opencast mining began in parishes where the red crag outcropped along the banks of the Orwell and Deben estuaries. Lawes, Colchester, Packard and Fison provided relatively well-paid employment for hundreds of local people in the digging, washing, sorting and transporting of Suffolk coprolites as well as in their manure factories and agency offices. (Buckland, op.cit. pp.520-21) Henslow reported to one of the manure manufacturers in the area that at Felixstow

> "*...We saw 1,000 tons lying in one field, and 1,000 more had been raised during the past winter. This is independent of the many thousand tons raised by Mr Lawes. Raised at 8 - 10s. a ton, sold at 24s. a ton. Manufactured phosphate sold at £7 a ton.*"

(Henslow, J.S. op.cit. p.520)

After paying the landowner for the right to dig, often a few shillings for every ton, Lawes could realise profits of up to 200%. Once transport and processing costs were deducted there was even more profit to be made when he sold superphosphate at £7.00 a ton. This was especially so when guano sold at £12.00 per ton. Landowners, farmers and labourers alike experienced the financial rewards from a new industry. Landowners received their royalties per ton and farmers were compensated for the land out of cultivation. Coprolite labourers made up to double the wages of agricultural labourers.

This spirit of entrepreneurship led in 1846 to a similar bed of "coprolites" being exploited from the Cambridgeshire fens, northeast of Cambridge. As they had slightly higher phosphate content than the Suffolk "coprolites" William Colchester decided to expand his operations into Cambridgeshire following a deal with a local doctor. He bought eleven acres for £1,000, many times their agricultural value. He went into partnership with Mr Ball, the local miller and in time set up a new manure works at Burwell. Being on Burwell Lode it allowed shallow draft lighters to take their coprolite cargoes downstream on the Cam to Littleport and then down the Ouse to King's Lynn. From here they were transhipped to works in Ipswich, London and elsewhere. (Rothamsted Archives, Letter from Henslow to Lawes' Lawyers, 10th June 1845; O'Connor, B. (1993), 'The Fenland Fossil Diggings' unpublished paper) Edward Packard followed suit. When the same seam was found exposed in the Lower Greensand above the Gault Clay in a Cambridge brickyard in 1849 Lawes expanded his interests in the area as the Cambridge Independent Press of 1851 indicates

> *"Brick-fields at Barnwell now yield a large supply, and contracts have been entered into at £20 per ton, £80 being given for the privilidge of digging over a field adjoining, to collect these exuviae of former life. An apparatus has been constructed for washing them on the spot; and from the proximity of the field to the railroad, they are deposited in trucks, and hundred of tons conveyed to the manufactory near London, where after calcination, they are ground and formed into a valuable artificial manure, equally rich as the costly guano in the fertilising principle of vegetation."*
>
> (Cambridge Independent Press, 18th Jan.1851 p3)

None of Lawes' agreements for these early "diggings", as they became known, have come to light. Gradually they spread piecemeal along the banks of the Cam where the Greensand outcropped above the gault clay. Although few of Lawes' personal papers have come to light, there is evidence that in the following decades he went on to make similar arrangements with Cambridgeshire and other landowners along the "coprolite belt".

## ADULTERATIONS AND ROYALTIES

In the late-1850s Lawes' Deptford factory was producing some 15,000 tons of superphosphate annually. What volume his competitors were making is uncertain neither is whether they were all paying him royalties. Potentially he was making many thousands of pounds every year out of these which irritated some competitors. As a result of his legal action Lawes was compelled to issue a disclaimer in February 1848. This removed the words bone and bone dust from his patent and he acknowledged both Murray's and Liebig's discoveries. (Rothamsted Archives, A2; Kiln, A. (1979), 'The Coprolite Industry', Putteridge Bury College, p.17) By March 1848 he had evidence that competitors were adulterating their superphosphate and not paying him his royalties. He asked Gilbert "*to visit Fisons in London to ask what scientific evidence they will be likely to require.* " Two of his employees were instructed to acquire some "super" from the London Manure Company, of Bridge Street, Blackfriars. Its analysis confirmed that they were infringing his patent. His wealth from both the coprolite and manure business allowed him to take on legal advisers who initiated action against their chairman, Mr Pursar. The case was put forward that the

> "*Plaintiff finding that large quantities of the Patented Manure were sold in competition with him in the market though generally of an inferior quality and adulterated with worthless materials felt it necessary to establish publicly the validity of his own Patent.*"
>
> (Rothamsted Archives, Patent Suit, A2.)

His advisers informed him that his patent had limitations and in a letter to Gilbert he acknowledged he was "*quite prepared to lose my lawsuit and therefore I cannot be disappointed*". He was aware that his patent suffered from the same problems as Murray's in that they were "*deficient in precision*". The instructions had to be clear enough so that a labourer in a chemical factory could make his manures without reference to a chemistry manual.

> "*...the argument was questionable as to whether Lawes' Patent would stand well in a trial - the imperfection being too obvious not to be taken advantage of by the scientific men engaged by the opponents who would also be aware that the coprolite and mineral bone even now in use could not have been contemplated by the patentee, their discovery being of a posterior date.*"

(Rothamsted Archives, A2)

Details of the case were reported in the agricultural press of 1851 as it was of great interest to many in the manure trade. The Mark Lane Express brought the following notice to its readers' attention.

> ***"SUPER PHOSPHATE OF LIME***
> *To Manufacturers, Dealers in and Consumers of Super phosphate of lime. At a Meeting of some of the principal Manufacturers and Dealers in super phosphate of lime held at the Green Dragon, Bishopsgate Street, on Monday 1st of March for the purpose of taking into consideration the propriety of resisting the attempts now making [sic] by Mr J.B. Lawes to establish an exclusive right to the manufacture and sale of this article, it was resolved unanimously, First, that this attempt be resisted by every justifiable means and, Second, that a subscription be entered into to assist in the defence of any Action that may be brought for the infringement of this presumed exclusive right to manufacture super phosphate of lime. Upward of £500 was subscribed in the room, nearly the whole of which has been paid into the hands of James Odams, 35 Leadenhall St., London, who was appointed Treasurer. Persons interested in upholding a fair and open Trade in this article are requested to communicate with Mr James Odams."*

(Mark Lane Express and Agricultural Journal, 8th March 1851)

To further frustrate Lawes and entangle him even more

in expensive legal expenses, Odams took out his own patent. (Rothamsted Archives, Patent Suit, pp.20-21) Although he lost the case Mr Pursar agreed to pay Lawes a ten shillings a ton royalty. After the trial Pursar's supporters presented him

> *"...with a plate to mark their sense of the so-called services he had rendered to the Trade and Agricultural Community by defending and proceeding to Trial with the action for the purpose of defeating the Plaintiff's patent."*
>
> (Ibid.)

Lawes took similar action against Edward Packard and Joseph Fison. Packard agreed to pay Lawes "*a considerable royalty*" but what happened with Fison has not come to light. One of the cases was held in Ipswich which, due to its continually being delayed, occasioned Rev. Henslow with considerable irritation. As president of the Ipswich Museum he alluded to it in his speech at the 1850 annual dinner.

> *"I was supposed to have said I had received a subpoena to attend a trial in which the sum of £7,000 was involved, in respect of the nodules, commonly called "coprolites," found in the neighbourhood of Felixstow. It will be seen by the sequel, that I must have said "£7,000 per annum." The trial to which I referred was brought to an issue last Monday, and the verdict was adverse to the claims of the plaintiff, who had taken out a patent, in 1842, for the manufacture of superphosphate of lime... A host of witnesses were subpoenaed, and among them I recognised at least seven Professors in Chemistry, Geology, Anatomy, etc. Considering the pains that had been taken with this case, and the great expense to which the opposing parties had been put themselves, it seems to me strange that the newspapers the following day should merely have*

*stated that, "the Exchequer Court had been occupied all day with a patent case which contained nothing of sufficient interest to be reported." I venture to believe the case will prove to have been one of interest to some of the landed proprietors of East Suffolk, and possibly some in Essex also, who happen to possess property on the red crag formation. I also think it is a case which might be adduced with success against some of the absurdities of our patent laws... The extent to which the nodules have already been raised is enormous, considering how short a time has elapsed since the spirit and energy of Mr Lawes were first brought to bear upon the question of their being made serviceable to the manufacture of superphosphate of lime. Hitherto, I understand, the demand has exceeded the supply; but the extent to which I am inclined to believe they may yet be procured is an hundredfold greater than I had ever before supposed to have been likely. It may afford some idea of the importance of these "diggings" when I state that I have been assured by those who appear to have possessed excellent opportunities of knowing the fact, that £10,000 per annum is within the income which has recently been derived from the sale of phosphate of lime obtained from these "diggings."*

(Suffolk Chronicle, 26th December, 1850)

Entrepreneurs would not have ignored such enormous profits with an eye for investment in the early fertiliser industry. Whilst the details Henslow gave may have restricted Lawes from capitalising further in the Suffolk area, it helps explain why he moved into Cambridgeshire. It also gave some of the local landowners an opportunity to develop their entrepreneurial skills. Henslow's contemporaries said that, being a man of the cloth, he did not wish to benefit financially from his discovery. He had an ulterior motive it seemed.

> *"...If any of the landed proprietors of the neighbourhood should profit by these hints, I may probably some day venture to remind them, cap in hand, that a small fragment of their gains might advantageously be appropriated to the funds of Ipswich Museum."*
>
> (Ibid.)

If it was Lawes that had made the £7,000 or even the £10,000 per annum from Suffolk one wonders what his income from the Cambridgeshire coprolites would have been. When one considers that £25 - £30 would have been the annual wages of an agricultural labourer at that time and £200 would have bought a small estate then Lawes was in another class altogether. His entry in the 1851 census described him as a 36-year old "*Gentleman,*" born in Harpenden and married to 28 year old Caroline with a son Charles and daughter, Caroline. He had a housekeeper, lady's maid, nurse, housemaid, kitchen maid, laundry maid, cook, dairymaid, vermin destroyer, footman, groom, bailiff and farm servant. (Herts. County Record Office (HCRO).1851 census Harpenden)

By the early 1850s there were twelve manure manufactories in Great Britain and the manure business was also expanding on the continent and in the United States. Interest in geology had sparked off surveys across Europe and phosphorite, a rock phosphate, was found in Estremadura in Spain in 1845. The following year it was found in the Ardennes and Pas de Calais in France. Apatite, another rock phosphate, was worked in Arendal in Norway and Pargas in Finland in 1851. With apatite mines opening in

Amberg in Bavaria, Ehrenfriedsdorf in Saxony and Schlackenwald in Bohemia also in 1851 Lawes and the other manure companies began importing increasing quantities. In the United States they were using guano and buffalo bones as fertiliser. But with the discovery of mineral phosphate of lime in New Jersey and New York which had a phosphate content of over 80% they were able to start manufacturing superphosphate from 1852. However, "coprolites" were still the major raw material of the British superphosphate.

As Henslow pointed out, Lawes' legal actions had stimulated intense interest in these new fossil beds. Although this led to the conclusion amongst Victorian geologists that the coprolites were not in fact fossilised droppings, the term coprolites remained as a trade name. This explains the confusion, even today, over their origin. Some real coprolites have been found in the bed in recent years, for example the Barrington coprolite and the flat-bottomed, sun-dried lumps from Sandy. The bed included an assortment of bones, teeth, scales and claws of dinosaurs that were wiped out about 90 million years ago. Geological literature referred to iguanodon, megalosaurus, craterosaurus, dakosaurus and dinotosaurus being unearthed in the fossil bed. There were also remains of marine reptiles - ichthyosaurus, pliosaurus and plesiosaurus and the bird pterodactyl. Fossils of whale, shark, turtle as well as numerous shells, sponges and other marine organisms were found. The most notable were ammonites - a member of the squid family. What had brought about this mass extinction? Suggesting there had been a massive inundation mixed amongst them were the fossil remains of land animals like elephant, hippopotamus, crocodile, horse, hyena and tapir. There is a suggestion that the mammal deposits were uncovered in more recent beds by the diggers as they searched for the more ancient deposits. It is thought that tectonic activity as the earth's plate moved towards their present position released vast quantities of flood basalts above magma plumes. Volcanic explosions gave off enormous clouds of volcanic dust and poisonous carbon dioxide and sulphur dioxide which changed the atmosphere. Global warming raised daytime temperatures and brought freezing winter conditions. The larger creatures experienced respiratory problems and died under the prolonged environmental stress. A huge inundation caused by rising sea levels during the Late Cretaceous led to large-scale extinctions. Submerged in shallow warm water the decomposing organisms became phosphatised on the seabed and then covered in subsequent deposits of chalk and clay. It also included large numbers of inorganic phosphatic nodules. (O'Connor, B. (1998), 'The Dinosaurs on Sandy Heath'; O'Connor, B. (1993), 'The Origins and Development of Great Britain's Coprolite Industry' Subterranea Britannica, Bulletin 29, pp.21-31)

The vast majority of the bed was unrecognisable as a fossil deposit given the amount of rolling and erosion they experienced on the seabed. The better specimens were sold for a few shillings to visiting scholars who "haunted" the pits or taken to fossil stalls on the local markets. Many shelves in museums across the country included Greensand fossils from these coprolite pits. Whilst the academics preferred to call them "pseudo-coprolites" or "phosphatic nodules" rather than fossilised droppings no-one denied their agricultural value. T.J Herapath in 1851 commented that these remains

> *"...are met with in such enormous quantities on the coasts of Suffolk, Norfolk and Essex, where several hundreds of persons are now actively employed in exhuming and collecting them, with the view to their future conversion into artificial manures. It is from these counties, indeed, that Mar.*

*Lawes of Rothamsted, obtains nearly the whole of the material he employs in the preparation of his well-known "coprolite manure;" and so extensive is the demand for this description of fertilizers for wheat and turnip growing lands, I am credibly informed, that several thousand tons of fossil bones, &c. are annually sold in this country under one form or another, and the consumption of them is daily and rapidly increasing.. The Suffolk crag being exceedingly rich in fossils, both as regards number and quality, and the expense of water-carriage to any part of the Eastern coastline being at the same time very trifling, this county offers peculiar advantages to those who are engaged in this branch of traffic."*

(Herapath, T.J. (1851), 'Some Observations on the Chemical Composition and Agricultural Value of the Fossil Bones and Pseudo-Coprolites of the Crag.' Journ.Royal Agric.Soc. pp.91.)

Lawes consolidated his domination of the superphosphate business by buying up Sir James Murray's company in 1852. He bought similar patents but at a cost. There was an important case in 1853 against Mr Batchelor which secured his monopoly of his patent. (Russell, (1966), 'A history of Agricultural Science in Gt. Britain 1620 - 1954', pp.144-5) Despite legal bills in excess of £10,000 he had to take out a second disclaimer. This time it was against using bone as a source of phosphate. (Alford, W.A.L., notes on Sir J. Murray, 10/11/1952, Lawes Chemical Manure Company documents, Reading University; Rothamsted Library Archive A2) Despite these setbacks, his work at Rothamsted gave him an international reputation. This in turn helped his manure business to expand and allowed him to amass an enormous fortune over the next three decades.

## EXPANDING THE MANURE BUSINESS

By 1854 the annual production at his Deptford factory had reached 30,000 tons and was steadily increasing. He felt that the business could only expand but there was not enough space to enlarge his Deptford works. Accordingly, in 1857 he bought a 100-acre plot of land on the north side of the Thames at Barking Creek. On this marshland site there was room for an integrated chemical manure works with his own acid plant capable of producing up to 200 tons of sulphuric acid a week. There was a row of terraced houses constructed for the labourers to rent as well as a public house - 'The Crooked Billet'. With both factories in operation, superphosphate production more than doubled to 65,000 tons per annum by 1860. At prices around £7.00 a ton one can see it was a profitable venture.

In the 1861 census Lawes was described as a "*Landed proprietor occupying farm of 454 acres, employing 22 men and 17 boys. Engaged in Scientific Agriculture and manufacture of artificial manures employing 140 men.*" This was apart from the eighteen domestic and other servants living in the Manor. (HCRO.1861 census Harpenden) He must have been very busy supervising his experiments at Rothamsted and at Craig House, Dalmelly in Scotland where he used to spend several months each year improving newly acquired estates as well as deer stalking and fly fishing. As well as working with the Royal Agricultural Society of Scotland he also found time to write papers for agricultural journals, one every forty days on average. He had to discuss the legal action against his competitors and attend meetings with landowners, land agents, surveyors and solicitors. This was as well as overseeing the accounts of his coprolite and manure businesses and his overseas investments that included ownership of a sugar cane plantation in

Queensland, Australia. (Dyke, G. op.cit. p.3)

The earliest documentation of Lawes obtaining a coprolite licence was not until 1862. He offered Cambridge City Corporation £30 an acre to work Coldham's Common. He hadn't done his homework as his bid was significantly lower than his competitors' and was duly rejected. Despite increasing his offer to £56 it was again refused. The Corporation gave the licence to Robert Ground who was prepared to pay them £150 an acre! (Cambs. CRO. Commons Committee Minutes 1861 -1864; O'Connor, B. (1998), "The Dinosaurs on Coldham's Common', own publication) However, in the same year he gained a licence from a landowner in Edworth, near Ashwell and another from Trinity College, Cambridge to work part of their estate in Shillington, near Hitchin. How much he paid was not recorded. (Documents in possession of Mar. Smyth, Edworth; Trinity College Muniments Shillington Box 6)

By 1864 evidence shows he gained a further licence in Cambridge. He paid St. John's College, Cambridge, £120 an acre, 400% more than he was prepared to pay three years earlier. This was to work part of the college's Barnwell estate near Coldham's Common. The proximity of the Great Eastern Railway to the Cambridgeshire "diggings" benefited Lawes greatly with reduced transport costs. He took on Luke Griffin as manager whose labourers worked almost nine acres over the next few years. (St. John's College Muniments Box Barnwell)

With more and more manure companies being established with new manure factories in the industrial urban centres there was a growing demand for coprolites. The "diggings" were on such a large scale by the mid-1860s that the solicitors acting for the landowners insisted upon a royalty per acre. This provided them as well as surveyors with valuable additional business. The cost of installing weigh houses at each site and the time wasted in weighing thousands of tons leaving each field was also a factor. This necessitated Lawes hiring the services of the Hitchin-based surveyor, George Beaver. He had to measure the workings twice a year to determine from the acreage worked the amount payable to the landowner.

Beaver's diaries showed Lawes had agreements in numerous villages along the coprolite belt and the list below shows just how extensive his operations were.

| | |
|---|---|
| Shillington, Beds. | 1862 |
| Edworth, Beds. | 1862 |
| Little Eversden, Cambs. | 1863 |
| Coldham's Common, Cambridge | 1864 |
| Dunton Lodge Farm, Beds. | 1868 |
| Guilden Morden, Cambs. | 1869 |
| Comberton, Cambs. | 1869 |
| Billington, Beds. | 1870 |
| Horningsea, Cambs. | 1870 |
| Hunsdon Lodge Farm, Stondon, Beds. | 1870 |
| Ashwell, Herts. | 1870 |
| Arlesey, Beds. | 1870 |
| Meldreth, Cambs. | 1871 |

(George Beaver's diaries, Hitchin Museum)

There were undoubtedly many more but with landowners whose records were never deposited in County Record Offices or whose solicitors and surveyors records still lay hidden away. In many parishes the "diggings“ lasted for many years as the trenches gradually stretched their way across the fields but in some, like Shillington, they lasted over 20 years.

Lawes had to take on an agent for particular areas; Joseph

Weston for the south-western area, Mar. Wyatt for the central area and Luke Griffin for the eastern area. Foremen were also taken on to supervise each diggings. They were responsible for hiring and firing and arranging the shipments of "coprolites" to his London works. His record books did not show that he made any coprolite purchases from other contractors. This would have maximised his profits, especially when he had also invested in the plant, tools and machinery at all the works. This equipment was transferred from site to site as the work progressed. In fact there were no records of any of Lawes coprolite plant being put up for sale.

In 1865 Lawes was reputed to be clearing between £40,000 to £50,000 annually. (Rothamsted pamphlets 7, 18) This was a phenomenal sum in those days. Aware of the dangers of specialisation, he diversified into other manufactures and the following year he took over the Atlas Chemical Works in Millwall. These works he improved to produce tartaric and citric acid - raw materials for the food manufacturing industry. In 1869 the British Chemical and Agricultural Manure Company set up a factory on the side of the Thames close to Lawes' Deptford site. Whether Lawes had any connection with this company is unclear.

Documents in Rothamsted Archive shed light on his involvement in the coprolite industry during 1867.

*Mill Field No 1 Eversden*
*£27 11s. 9d was paid for levelling.*

*Mill Field 2 Eversden*
*Between 1st July and 31st December 1867, Lawes' labourers raised 176 tons 6 cwt. at a cost of £305 6s. 1½d. This included £191 18s. labour costs, £57 10s. royalty to the Earl of Hardwick and £66 17s. for carriage*

*to Deptford. This averaged £2 1s. 3d per ton.*

*Apsley End*
*Between 1st July and 31st December 1867, Lawes' labourers raised 993 tons 15 cwt. at a cost of £2,173 2s. 4d. This included £1,200 16s. 8d. labour costs, £223 11s. 10½d. royalty at 4s. 6d. a ton, £2 10s. for well cleaning and boring, £99 7s. 6d. for coals at 2s a ton, £37 5s, 4d for levelling at 9d. a ton and £356 1s. 10½d. for carriage to Deptford.. This averaged £2 3s. 8½d. per ton.*

*Dunton*
*Between 1st July and 31st December 1867, Lawes' labourers raised 965 tons 15 cwt. at a cost of £2,250 10s. 7½d This included £1,445 15s. 11½d. labour costs, washing at 9s. per ton, carting at 2s. 3d. per ton, £241 8s. 9d royalty at 5s. a ton, £2 18s. for boring, £72 8s. 7½d for coals at 1s. 6d. a ton, £48 5s, 9d for levelling at 1s. a ton and £404 7s. 11d. for carriage to Deptford.. This averaged £2 6s. 7½d. per ton.*

*St John's No1 (Most probably on Coldham's Common)*
*£39 16s. 10d was paid for levelling.*

*St John's No. 2*
*Between 1st July and 31st December 1867, Lawes' labourers raised 291 tons at a cost of £819 4s. 2d This included £502 7s. 8½d. labour costs, £110 6s. 9d royalty to Mr Reyner at 6s. a ton, £29 12s. for coals at 2s. a ton, £9 14s. for levelling at 8s. a ton and £110 6s. 9d. for carriage to Deptford.. This averaged £2 16s. 3½d. per ton.*

*St John's No. 3*
*Between 1st July and 31st December 1867, Lawes' labourers raised 441 tons at a cost of £1,150 18s. 5d This*

*included £669 18s. 6d. labour costs, £176 8s. royalty to Mr Reyner at 8s. a ton, £44 2s. for coals at 2s. a ton, £14 14s. for levelling at 8s. a ton and £167 4s. 3d. for carriage to Deptford.. This averaged £2 12s. 4d. per ton.*

*Potton*

*Between 1st July and 31st December 1867, Lawes' labourers raised 849 tons of large coprolites and 106 tons of smalls at a cost of £974 15s. 5½d. This included £424 17s. 8½d. labour costs, £100. royalty to Sir Burgoyne and £30 for carting 720 tons to Potton Station at 10s.a ton. A Mr Godden was paid £10 14s, 3½d salary for three months and Mr Weston was paid ££7 10s. 0d. for six months. The average price at Potton Station was £1 2s. 0d. per ton.*

*Higham Gobion*

*Between 1st July and 31st December 1867, Lawes' labourers at Higham Gobion had raised an estimated 300 tons. None were sold as the washmill needed fixing. The costs were £92 7s. 5d. which included £28 10s. 8d. labour costs for fixing the mill, £50 royalty to Mr Passingham, £7 10s. 0d. salary to Mr Weston, £5 0s.9d. tradesmen's bills and £1 6s. 0d. incidental expenses.*

*Arlesey*

*Between 1st July and 31st December 1867, Lawes' labourers at Arlesey had raised an estimated 160 tons but none were sold as the washmill had not been erected. The costs were £390 0s. 8d. which included £107 0s. ½d. labour costs, £100. royalty to Mr Edwards, £120 0s. 4d.capital on equipment, £28 6s.3½d. tradesmen's bills, £12 for sinking a well. Mr Weston was paid ££7 10s. 0d. for six months with £15 travelling costs.*

*Shillington*

*Between 1st July and 31st December 1867, Lawes costs at Shillington were £195 7s. 9½d. This included labour costs of £139 14s.9½d for levelling the coprolite pits. Mr Rumball was paid £55 13s.0d. for levelling and valuing the damage to the land between 1863 and 1866. Mr Musgrave was also paid £80.*

(Rothamsted Research: Archives B8.3)

Such was the success of superphosphate, however, that by 1870 he had fifteen agents across the country with a Head Office at 59 Mark Lane, London. He had branches in Wales, Scotland, Ireland and the Channel Islands and traded overseas in North and South America, India, New Zealand, Australia, South Africa, and the Middle East. The 1871 census showed that, now aged 56, he was a "*Landowner, manufacturer of artificial manures, tartaric acid, citric acid and Scientific Farmer.*" With his children grown up he only had need for fourteen servants. (HCRO.1871 census, Harpenden)

Further insight into his coprolite business came as a result of an enquiry in 1871 by the Agricultural Gazette and Gardeners' Chronicle. It was a publication which commanded wide readership amongst the nation's agriculturalists and, given, the profitability of the diggings, may well have stimulated further contracts. It also brought the industry to the nation's attention. A delegation from the paper visited his works in Shillington during the winter, the busiest part of the year.

***SHILLINGTON.*** *It was to some of Mar. LAWES' workings that we paid a visit last week, and his experience may be quoted for the information of those who believe that they have coprolites in their land. This belief may have arisen when some of the* *characteristic fossils having been found within the soil, or having been turned up when digging drains. The first step is to examine the field by borings. There is a tool for the purpose, a sort of taster, by which a 2-inch boring of the subsoil can be brought up from any depth, of 2 to 20 feet. Such borings should be made at ten yard intervals all over the suspected area, and if the existence of these coprolites is revealed by them, the layer must be uncovered here and there, perhaps in three or four places in a ten acre field, and the quantity of the coprolites ascertained by washing a square yard or two of the layer, taking up its whole thickness for the purpose. But indeed, if the owner has ascertained the existence of a bed of sufficient richness, all this somewhat expensive process will be done for him by the purchaser. He may thus ascertain how many tons of coprolite he may expect per acre, and the depth from which they have to be dug.*

*The buyer will offer a price according to these two factors in the valuation. He will make a contract with the tenant also, engaging to complete the work of extraction in three or perhaps four years, undertaking to level the moved subsoil and replace the soil, leaving everything as he found it, and paying a certain sum per acre for the lost profits of the occupation. The contract with the landlord specifies the purchase-money varying from £60 to £100 or more per acre, according to the ascertained productiveness of the bed, and the estimated cost of working it.*

*When these particulars are settled, the purchaser proceeds to work the field he sinks and bores a well, getting through the gault into a water-bearing stratum. He sets up an 8 or 10 horse-power engine in a shed near the well, and thence pumps sufficient -*

*say 30 or 40 gallons a minute - into a horizontal washing mill, into which and out of which this water continually pours. The mill itself is a circular ring trough, perhaps of nearly 14 feet outer and 9 feet inner radius, thus providing a circular bed less than five feet wide and 3 or 4 feet deep, into which it may be up to 100 trucks of the dug up stratum of coprolites are tilted, one in every five or six minutes, throughout the day. A pair of heavy, long tined iron drags within this trough are continually driven round and round, by proper mill gearing, worked by the steam engine, and the muddy water, laden with the clayey matter thus discharged, is constantly pouring from it, leaving the hard nodules in the bottom of the trough. After 60 or 70 loads have been thus tilted in, the water is allowed to run clean. Three such washings, each of four tons weight or thereabouts, may be got out in two days. In one field at Shillington, near Hitchin, there were three such mills at work, and 100 tons a-week were being got - about 170 men and boys being at work. The diggings here are very deep, and the costs in this case probably are larger in excess of the average.*

*While the mill is being erected a party of men commence digging down to the bed, clearing, it may be, from 6 to 10 feet width, according to the depth of the layer, along one side of the area. We know of no workings more than 18 feet deep. If the stratum is deeper than that, it does not pay to lift, unless indeed it be unusually productive. The "rid" or waste top layers is in the first instance removed to a piece of land hired to receive it, the top soil being kept separate for replacement; but the next slice of land, yard by yard, is thrown forward into the trench dug out, the top soil for a width of perhaps 30 yards being put in barrows and wheeled into a ridge along the top of the first moved slice of subsoil. When 30 yards in width of the field has been dug over and the stratum dug out has accumulated in a heap beside the mill, the next 30 yards is skinned; and, the soil being placed in another ridge parallel with the first along the nearest line of moved subsoil, the interval of roughly turned over subsoil between the two ridges becomes a "pane", on which the washings of the mill can be poured. The washing then commences. Clean water is pumped into the mill, and the muddy stream is pumped from it, and by troughing is conveyed evenly over the surface of this interval until another space is ready, which in its turn receives its share. In this way then the whole field is cleared, dug over perhaps 5 feet, perhaps 15 feet deep. The coprolites, washed out and picked over, are weighed into the nearest railway trucks; the mud washed from them is evenly spread over the intervals between the parallel ridges of moved soil; and the whole, after a summer's drying is ready to be levelled back again. This may cost from £8 to £14 an acre... The farmer gets his land restored to him with the subsoil deeply stirred, and the soil relaid evenly; the wells are filled up, and the machinery removed to other diggings, and the land is left better than it was before. The landlord has meanwhile had perhaps the double of its agricultural value put in his pocket; an army of labourers - and a capital set of fellows they looked, the Cambridgeshire quarrymen, or navvies, in Mar. WESTON'S employment, under Mar. LAWES at Shillington - have earned their 15s. a-week apiece during the winter months; and the tenant has had an easier earned farm profit (with his rent paid for him) than any other field given him. Moreover, the land is improved without expense to him. We saw a large stubble field, on which manure*

The Distribution of Great Britain's Coprolite Industry 1842 - 1904

Undated photograph of John Bennet Lawes
http://www.rothamsted.ac.uk/Content/Library/Images/LawesStudioPhotoSmall.jpg

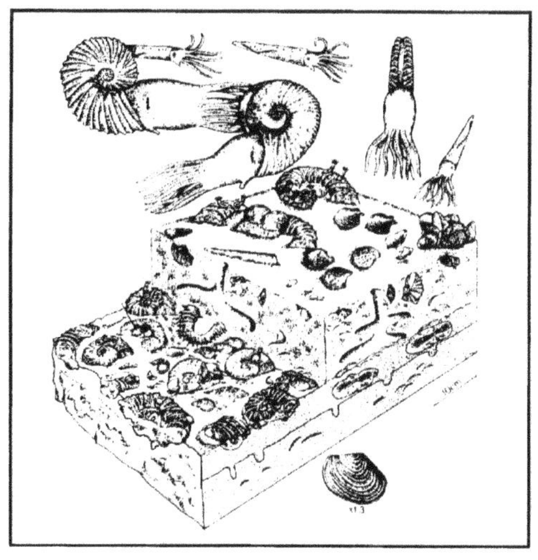

The Phosphate Bed Community
(McKerrow, W.S. (1978), *'The Ecology of Fossils An Illustrated Guide'*, Duckworth, p.286)

**Lower Cretaceous Terrestrial Communities**
a *Iguanadon* (Vertebrata: Reptilia: Archosaur – dinosaur)
b *Megalosaurus* (Vertebrata: Reptilia: Archosaur – dinosaur)
c *Hypsilophodon* (Vertebrata: Reptilia: Archosaur – dinosaur)
d *Acanthopholis* (Vertebrata: Reptilia: Archosaur – dinosaur)
e *Equisetites* (Pteridophyta: Calamites – horsetails)

The Phosphate Community
(McKerrow, W.S. (1978), *'The Ecology of Fossils An Illustrated Guide'*, Duckworth, p.286)

Felixstow (Suffolk) coprolites
(Courtesy of Earth Sciences Museum, Cambridge)

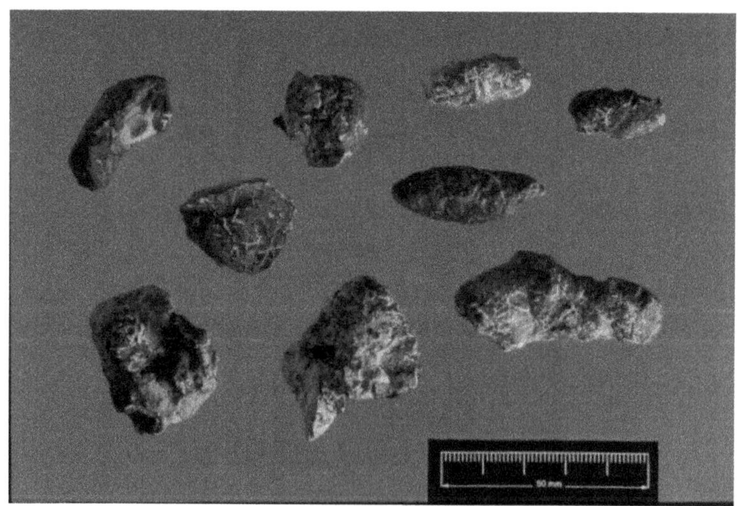

Cambridgeshire coprolites
(Courtesy of Earth Sciences Museum, Cambridge)

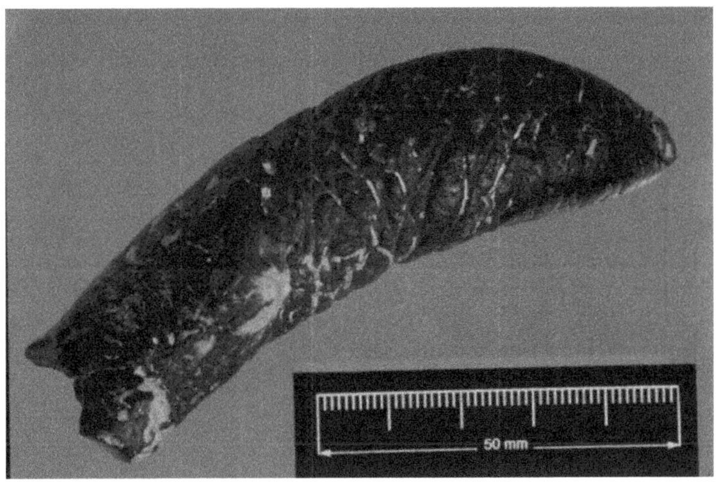


The Barrington coprolite
(Photograph courtesy of Earth Sciences Museum, Cambridge)

Bedfordshire coprolites
(Courtesy of Earth Sciences Museum, Cambridge)

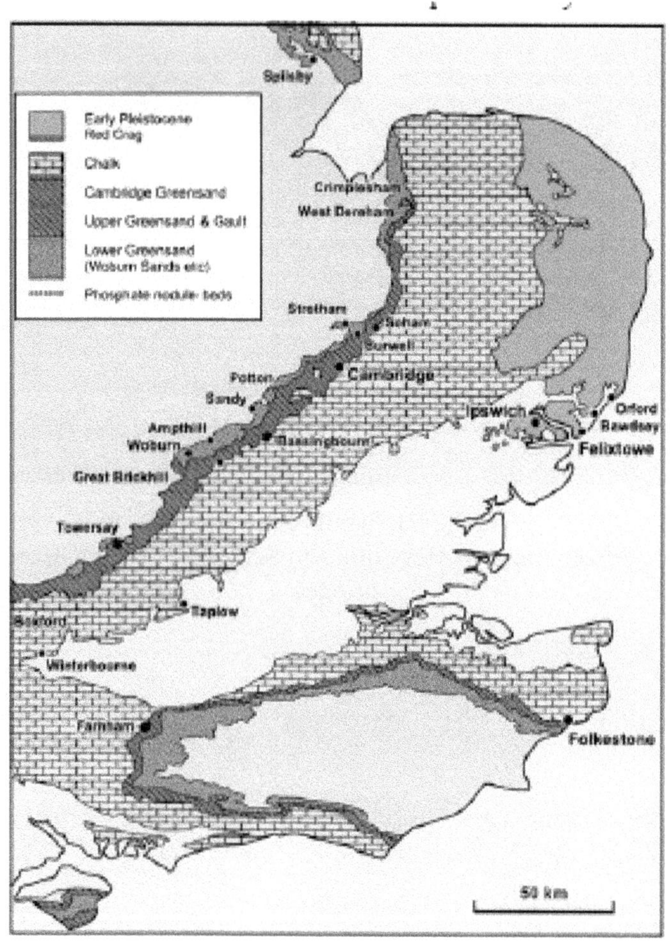


The main outcrops of the coprolite bearing beds within the Lower Greensand, Gault Clay and Red Crag series. (Ford, T. and O'Connor, B. 'A Vanished Industry: Coprolite Mining,' *Mercian Geologist*, 2009, p.96)

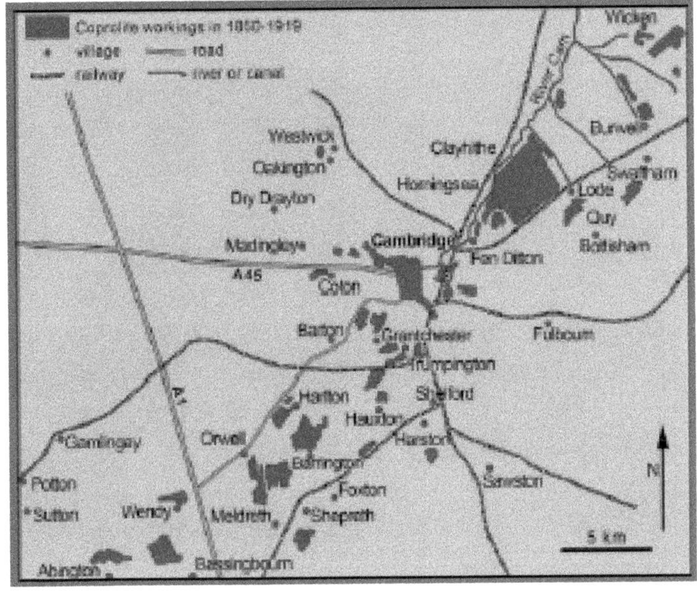


Coprolite workings around Cambridge (after map in Grove, R. (1976), 'The Cambridgeshire Coprolite Mining Rush, Oleander Press, Cambridge)

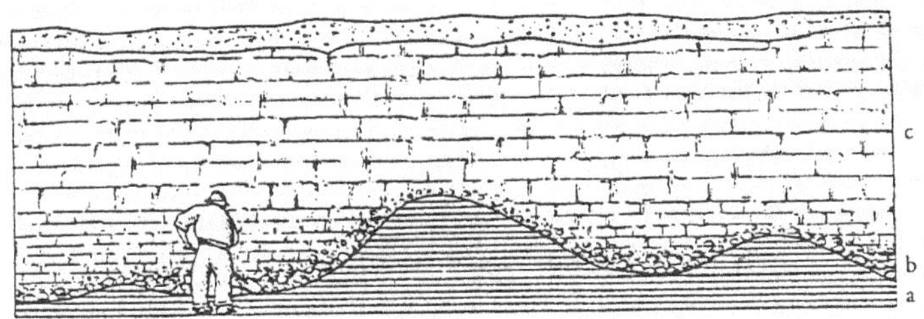


View of a coprolite pit in Horningsea, Cambs.
(Jukes-Browne, A.J. & Hill, W. *Cretaceous Rocks of Britain,* Mem. Geol. Surv. 1903, p.194)

Undated photograph of guano workings on Chincha Island, Peru. The deposits were up to 80 feet (29.6 m.) thick. (Clayton, A. (1985), *W.R. Grace & Co. The Formative years,* Jameson Books, Illinois)

Undated sketch of French coprolite works. L'exploitation des nodules phosphatés des Sables verts de la Meuse et des Ardennes au XIXe siècle, qui a conduit à la découverte de nombreux restes de vertébrés albiens. D'après Stansislas Meunier.

1887 photograph of a horse-drawn coprolite tumbril (cart) and washing pit on the banks of the River Deben beside what is now Waldringfield Sailing Club, Suffolk. (Suffolk Photographic Survey, Abbot's Hall Museum).

Horses, men and boy working at the coprolite washing pit beside the River Deben at Waldringfield. (Suffolk Photographic Survey, Abbot's Hall Museum).

Coprolite wheelbarrow on the plank which probably led up to a barge. The large front wheel allowed the workers to see the plank in front of them. (Suffolk Photographic Survey, Abbot's Hall Museum).

Coprolite Diggings in Cow Pasture, Abington Pigotts, Cambridgeshire, 1883
(Courtesy of Mr and Mrs Sclater, Abington Pigotts)

Coprolite Diggings at Orwell, Cambridgeshire. 1860s – 1870s
(Courtesy of Cambridgeshire Collection W27.1J80 25358)

http://www.rothamsted.ac.uk/Content/Library/Images/LawesSketchCroppedSmall.jpg

Coprolite workings at Brickhill, Bedfordshire in 1880s (Arthur Bates, Aylesbury

Undated postcard of horse-drawn tumbrils carrying coprolites to the railway station at Millbrook, Bedfordshire.

Photographs of the coprolite works on Sandy Heath, Bedfordshire, c.1882) The top photo shows women outside the sorting shed. The lower photographs shows a horse-powered cylindrical washmill. (Courtesy of Potton History Society)

Steam engine hauling coprolites from Whaddon to Shepreth Station c.1880 (Cambridge Collection Q AR J8 11029 Courtesy of Mrs Conings-by, Whaddon)

Suffolk coprolite washing. A long, water-filled trench was dug from the river and the coprolites were washed in wooden trays before being shovelled out into a pile. The brushwood fence protected the workers from the cold wind. (Suffolk Photographic Survey, Abbot's Hall Museum).

HORSE-POWERED COPROLITE WASHMILL

WOODEN ARM
POST
CHAINS ATTACHED TO HARROW
WATER PUMPED IN FROM ARTESIAN, OTHER WELL OR LODE
CIRCULAR IRON TRAY
WORKMAN WHEELING FOSSILS UP TO WASHMILL
WIMPOLE TREE
HORSE OPERATING THE HARROW
SLURRY OR SLUB PIT TO COLLECT, DIRTY WATER
BASED ON SKETCH IN RICHARD GROVE'S 'CAMBRIDGESHIRE COPROLITE MINING RUSH'

Washmill commonly used in Cambridgeshire, Bedfordshire, Norfolk and Buckinghamshire. (Based on sketch in Richard Grove's Cambridgeshire Coprolite Mining Rush)

Rothamsted Manor, home of John Bennet Lawes and the world's first agricultural research station.
http://www.hertfordshire-genealogy.co.uk/images/!/h/harpenden/

The barn at Rothamsted where Lawes' "super" was first made. A pond outside was where his labourers could wash off splashes of sulphuric acid.

Inside Lawes' barn at Rothamsted where his 'super' experiments took place. Notice the huge carboys of vitriol (sulphuric acid) (Courtesy of Rural History Centre, Reading University, Lawes Collection No. 43)

LAWES' MANURE FACTORY, DEPTFORD CREEK.

Lawes' Chemical Manure Company, Deptford Creek, established in 1843 (Spring Circular for Lawes' Manures 1864, Rural History Centre, Reading University)

(Courtesy of Lawes Agricultural Trust, Rothamsted Agricultural Station)

(Courtesy of Lawes Agricultural Trust, Rothamsted Agricultural Station)

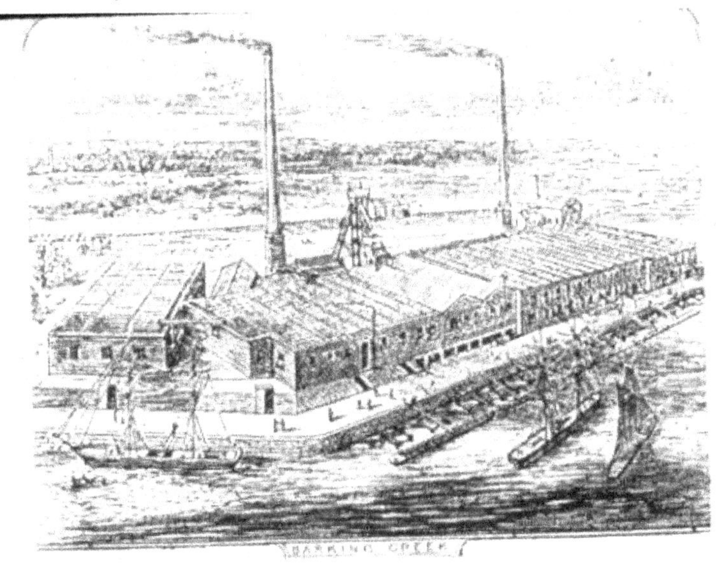

(Courtesy of Lawes Agricultural Trust, Rothamsted Agricultural Station)

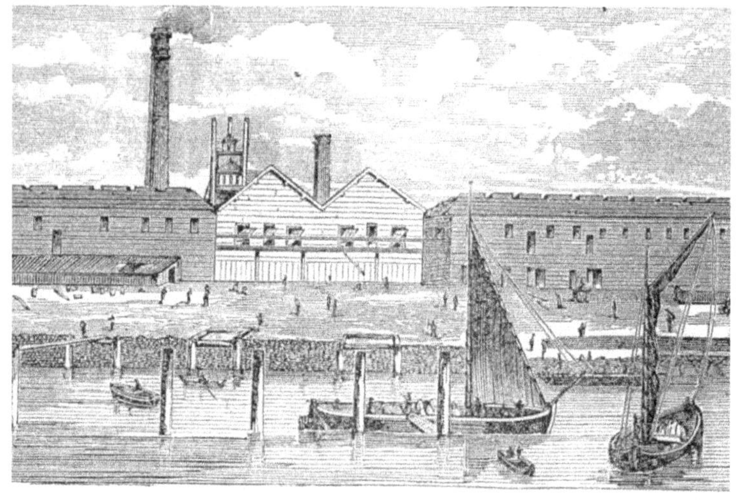

(Courtesy of Lawes Agricultural Trust, Rothamsted Agricultural Station)

Undated photograph of coprolites being unloaded at one of Lawes Chemical Manure Works on the Thames.
(Courtesy of Lawes Agricultural Trust, Rothamsted Agricultural Station)

OS map extract showing location of Lawes Chemical Manure Factory, Barking Creek

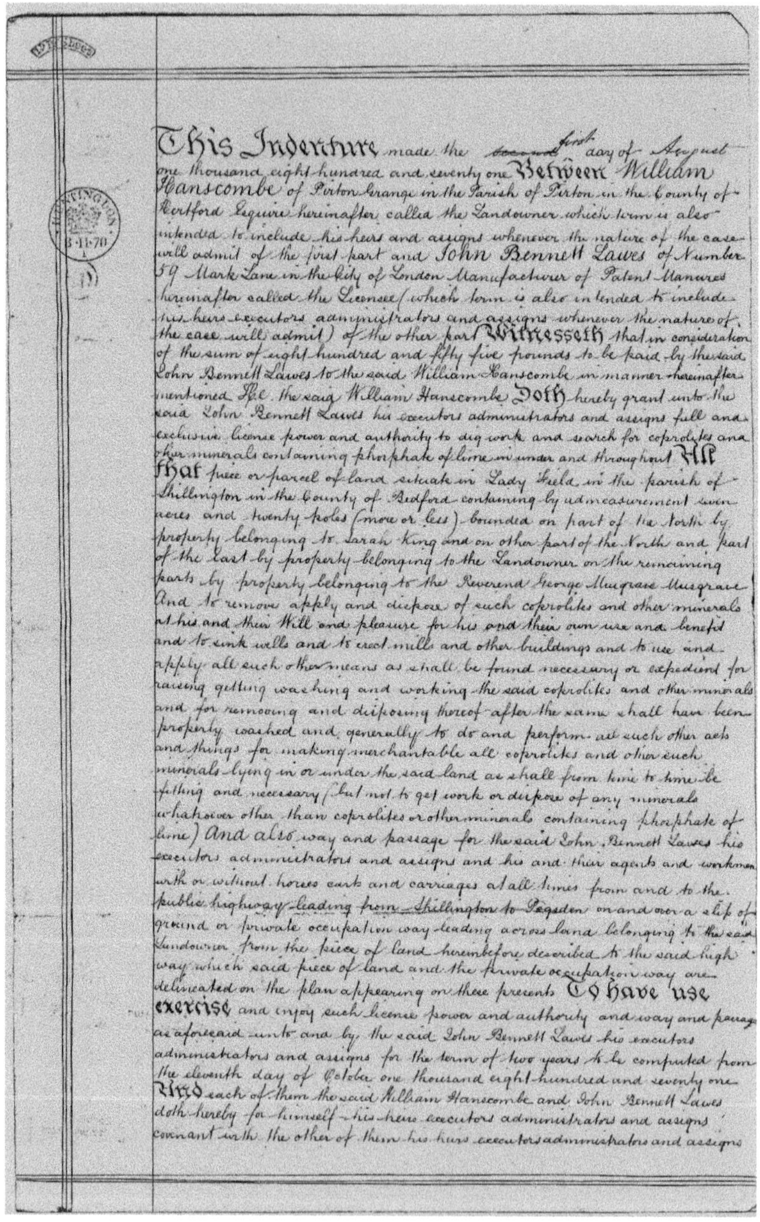

This Indenture made the ~~second~~ first day of August one thousand eight hundred and seventy one Between William Hanscombe of Pirton Grange in the Parish of Pirton in the County of Hertford Esquire hereinafter called the Landowner which term is also intended to include his heirs and assigns whenever the nature of the case will admit of the first part and John Bennett Lawes of Number 59 Mark Lane in the City of London Manufacturer of Patent Manures hereinafter called the Licensee (which term is also intended to include his heirs executors administrators and assigns whenever the nature of the case will admit) of the other part Witnesseth that in consideration of the sum of eight hundred and fifty five pounds to be paid by the said John Bennett Lawes to the said William Hanscombe in manner hereinafter mentioned He the said William Hanscombe Doth hereby grant unto the said John Bennett Lawes his executors administrators and assigns full and exclusive license power and authority to dig work and search for coprolites and other minerals containing phosphate of lime in under and throughout All that piece or parcel of land situate in Lady Field in the parish of Shillington in the County of Bedford containing by admeasurement seven acres and twenty poles (more or less) bounded on part of the North by property belonging to Sarah King and on other part of the North and part of the East by property belonging to the Landowner on the remaining parts by property belonging to the Reverend George Musgrave Musgrave And to remove apply and dispose of such coprolites and other minerals at his and their will and pleasure for his and their own use and benefit and to sink wells and to erect mills and other buildings and to use and apply all such other means as shall be found necessary or expedient for raising getting washing and working the said coprolites and other minerals and for removing and disposing thereof after the same shall have been properly washed and generally to do and perform all such other acts and things for making merchantable all coprolites and other such minerals lying in or under the said land as shall from time to time be fitting and necessary (but not to get work or dispose of any minerals whatsoever other than coprolites or other minerals containing phosphate of lime) And also way and passage for the said John Bennett Lawes his executors administrators and assigns and his and their agents and workmen with or without horses carts and carriages at all times from and to the public highway leading from Shillington to Pegsden on and over a slip of ground or private occupation way leading across land belonging to the said Landowner from the piece of land hereinbefore described to the said high way which said piece of land and the private occupation way are delineated on the plan appearing on these presents To have use exercise and enjoy such license power and authority and way and passage as aforesaid unto and by the said John Bennett Lawes his executors administrators and assigns for the term of two years to be computed from the eleventh day of October one thousand eight hundred and seventy one And each of them the said William Hanscombe and John Bennett Lawes doth hereby for himself his heirs executors administrators and assigns covenant with the other of them his heirs executors administrators and assigns

First page of Lawes' agreement with Hanscombe to raise coprolites in Shillington, Bedfordshire

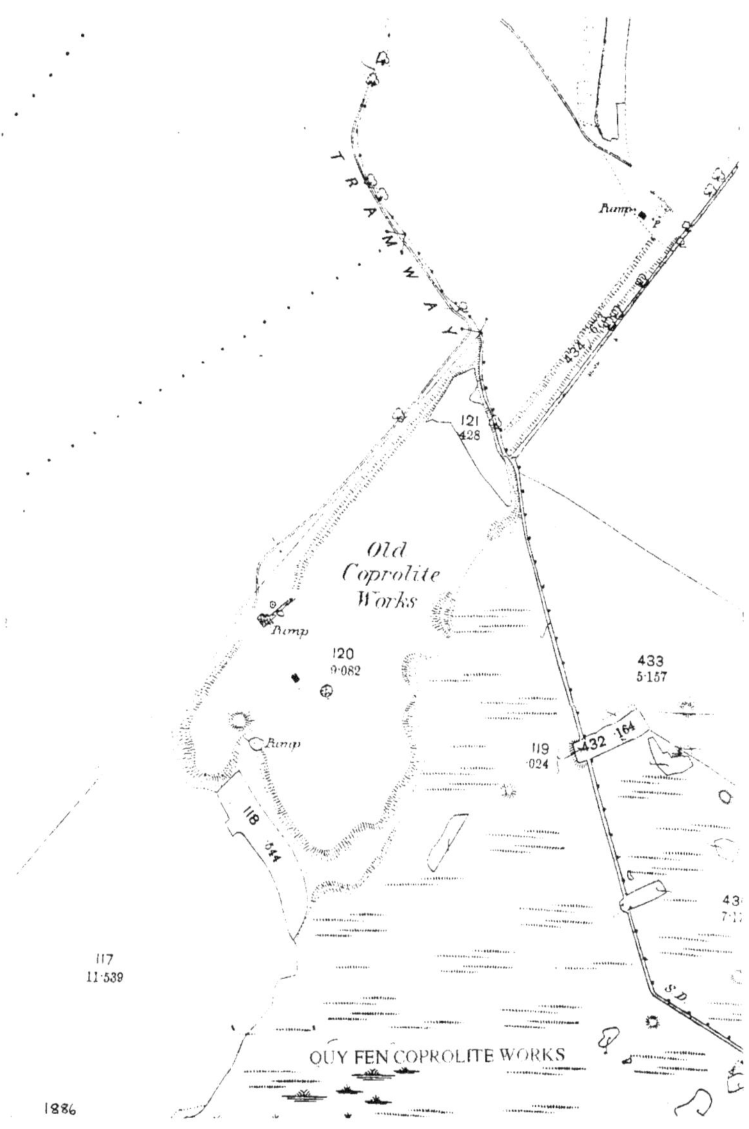


25” First edition OS map extract of the disused coprolite workings on Quy Fen. Note the tramway, pump and shed. Several water-filled pits can be seen and the sites of the washing mill.

# CAMBRIDGESHIRE.

PARTICULARS OF SALE WITH PLAN

OF A PECULIARLY

## VALUABLE ESTATE

THE WHOLE

TITHE FREE AND NEARLY ALL FREEHOLD,

IN THE PARISHES OF

HORNINGSEA AND BOTTISHAM,

CONSISTING OF

**509a. 1r. 37p.**

OF ARABLE, PASTURE, MEADOW, AND FEN

## LAND

IN TWO FARMS,

AND KNOWN AS THE

EYE HALL & CLAYHITHE FARMS,

WITH SUITABLE

RESIDENCES, AGRICULTURAL BUILDINGS, & LABOURERS' COTTAGES,

ALSO A

FULL TRADE BRICK YARD.

A CONSIDERABLE PORTION OF THE LAND CONTAINS

FINE VEINS OF COPROLITES,

AND THERE IS SOME GOOD BRICK EARTH.

The whole with the

**VALUABLE TIMBER**

Will be sold in One Lot, by Auction, by

## WISBEY AND SON

**On SATURDAY, MAY 28, 1870, at 5 o'clock in the Evening,**

*At the RED LION HOTEL, Petty Cury, Cambridge,*

By order of the Trustees for Sale under the Will of the late WILLIAM SAUNDERS, Esq., of Horningsea,

*The Farms are in the occupation of the Family of the late Mr. Saunders; and all the Tenants are under notice to quit at Michaelmas next.*

**To Test the Land for Coprolites application must be made to the Auctioneers.**

*Horningsea is about 4 Miles from Cambridge, and the Bottisham part of the Estate is immediately at the back of the Horningsea property.*

Further Particulars may be known of Messrs. EADEN, HARRIS, and KNOWLES, Solicitors, Cambridge; of Mr. JOHN WATTS, Solicitor, Bullock Market, St. Ives, Hunts.; Mr. J. W. PRIOR, Solicitor, Emmanuel Street, Cambridge; and of the Auctioneers, also of Cambridge.

W. METCALFE, PRINTER, GREEN STREET, CAMBRIDGE.

Sale Particulars of Eye Hall and Clayhithe Farms 1870
(CCRO. 132/M40)

# POOR'S FEN, QUY,

*CAMBS.*

CATALOGUE OF ALL THE VALUABLE

# COPROLITE PLANT

COMPRISING

About 20 tons of Tramway Rails, 40 Barrows, 10 Trucks, 70 Planks, 60 long Slurry Troughs, 40 Hoisting Frames, 25 Crowbars, 10 large Tubs and Tanks, Washing Mill and Slurry Wheel, complete,

**2 WELL-BUILT ENGINE HOUSES,**

**2 TIMBER-BUILT STABLES,**

**LARGE MESS ROOM,**

AND

**5 in. and 7 in. Centrifugal Pumps,**

**CAPITAL 10-H.P. PORTABLE ENGINE,**

Quantity of Cast-iron Piping, 6 Driving Straps, and numerous other Effects,

WHICH MESSRS.

# WRIGHT AND SCRUBY

Are instructed to sell by Auction, upon the Works, close to Quy Station, G.E.R.

*ON TUESDAY, OCTOBER 30th, 1894,*

At Eleven o'clock in the Morning.

Catalogues may be obtained of the A[illegible]IONEERS, Cambridge and March.

*J. Webb & Co., Printers, Alexandra Street, Cambridge.*

Sale particulars of the Quy Fen coprolite plant
(CCRO.R89/40 Francis papers)

http://www.rothamsted.ac.uk/Content/Library/Images/Manure%20Ad2.jpg

John Bennet Lawes

Popular Science Monthly | Volume 28 | March 1886

Caricature of John Bennet Lawes who patented the use of coprolites as an artifical manure in 1842 (*Vanity Fair* 8th July

PUNCH'S FANCY PORTRAITS.—No. 87.

SIR JOHN BENNET LAWES, BART.

THE AGRICULTURAL LAWES, THE NEW WHEEL-BARROW-NET.
*MOTTO, "LAUS ET HONOR."*

Punch, or the London Charivari, June 10 1882

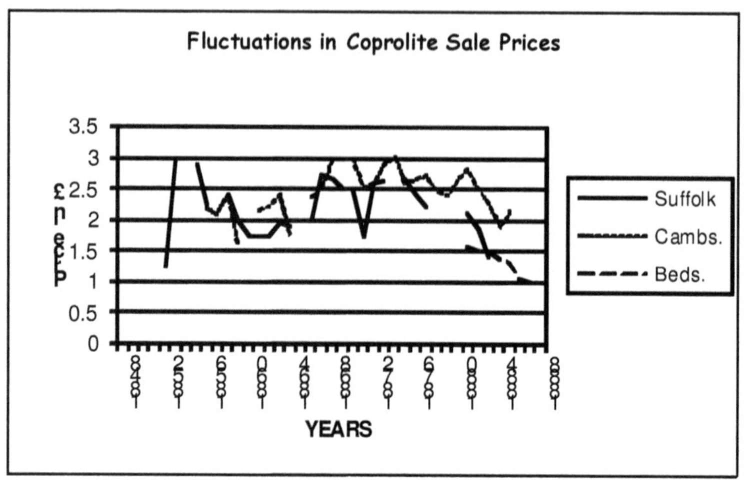


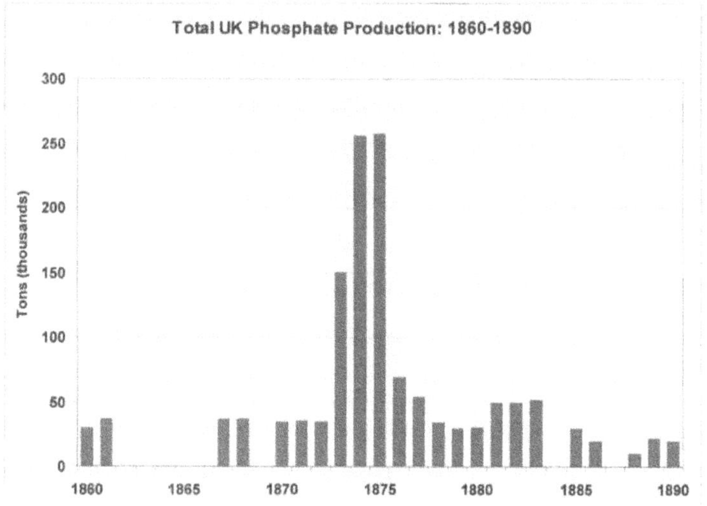


**Data from Parliamentary Accounts of 1891 Source: *The Cambridgeshire Coprolite Mining Rush*, Richard Grove, 1976**

Cambridgeshire was producing practically all raw material phosphate for fertiliser in Britain.

Phosphate workers at Charleston, South Carolina, United States (Unknown source)

Phosphate workers at Charleston, South Carolina, United States (Unknown source)

Phosphate mill at Charleston Mining Company's works
(Frank Leslie's Illustrated Newspaper June 30th 1877)

Phosphate mill at Charleston Mining Company's works
(*Frank Leslie's Illustrated Newspaper* ,June 30th 1877)

THE MARK LANE EXPRESS AND AGRICULTURAL JOURNAL, MAY 20, 1872.

# LAWES' CHEMICAL MANURE COMPANY (LIMITED).

INCORPORATED UNDER THE COMPANIES ACTS, 1862 AND 1867.

CAPITAL £600,000, IN 60,000 SHARES OF £10 EACH,

Of which it is proposed to CALL UP £8 ONLY, viz., £1 on Application, £3 on Allotment, £2 on 1st September, £2 on 1st December, 1872.

Shareholders may pay up £8, and will in that case be allowed Five per Cent. interest on the amount paid in advance of Calls.

NOT LESS THAN FIVE SHARES WILL BE ALLOTTED.

DIRECTORS.

JOHN KNOWLES (Chairman of Langdale's Chemical Manure Company, Limited), CHAIRMAN.
JAS. BARLOW, Manchester and Bolton, Spinner and Manufacturer.
SEPTIMUS BROWN, Newcastle, Russia Merchant (Director of Langdale's Chemical Manure Company, Limited).
WILLIAM COLCHESTER, Ipswich, Chemical Manure Manufacturer.
SAMPSON LANGDALE, Newcastle-upon-Tyne, Chemical Manure Manufacturer.
JAMES W. PORTER, Newcastle-upon-Tyne (Director of Langdale's Chemical Manure Company, Limited).
THOMAS VICKERS, Manchester, Manure Manufacturer.

BANKERS.

NATIONAL PROVINCIAL BANK OF ENGLAND, London, Manchester, Newcastle-upon-Tyne, and Branches.
BRITISH LINEN COMPANY, Edinburgh, Glasgow, and Branches.
NATIONAL BANK, Dublin and Branches.

SOLICITORS.

MESSRS. HALL & JANION, Solicitors, Manchester.

AUDITOR.

CHARLES TATTERSALL, Accountant, Manchester and London.

SECRETARY.

ROBERT P. WORRALL.

TEMPORARY OFFICES.—{LONDON: 26, MARK LANE.
MANCHESTER: 14, MARSDEN STREET.

PROSPECTUS.

This Company is formed to purchase and carry on the extensive Chemical Manure Manufactories and Business of Mr. John Bennet Lawes, of Rothamsted, Herts, and 59, Mark Lane, London.

This well-known business has been established upwards of 30 years, at the factories erected by Mr. Lawes, at Deptford and Barking Creek, on the Thames. The factory at Barking and the land belonging thereto is of freehold tenure, and contains nearly 100 acres, having a very extensive river frontage on the Thames and Creek.

The plant at Barking Creek consists of 43 vitriol chambers, producing about 20,000 tons of sulphuric acid yearly; a platinum still, for the production of oil of vitriol; three steam engines, with boilers; five pairs of millstones; Blake's Stone Crusher, Mixing and Disintegrating Machines, necessary plant for the extraction of sulphate of ammonia, an extensive wharf, with tramways, steam cranes, and other necessary and complete arrangements for discharging and loading ships.

There is also a manager's house, offices, and about fifty workmen's cottages.

The works at Deptford Creek comprise an extensive wharf and buildings, covering a considerable area, and are held for an unexpired term of about forty years, at a low rental.

The Plant consists of four steam engines, boilers, ten pairs of large millstones, powerful bone mills, dissolving machines, Blake's stone crusher, drying kilns, two Carr's disintegrators, and all other necessary gearing and machinery for conducting a most extensive business.

The Coprolite Works in Cambridgeshire and other counties consist of steam engines and washing mills, capable of producing about 12,000 tons of Coprolite yearly.

There are excellent offices in Mark Lane, held on very reasonable terms, and offices and extensive stores at Dublin, Shrewsbury, Cardiff, Bristol, Spalding, Exmouth, Ramsay, Aberdeen, and Leith.

The total sales of Manures and other articles connected with the trade show a progressive yearly increase of about 5,000 tons for the last three years.

In England, Scotland, and Ireland, exclusive of the islands, there are millions of acres of land not in cultivation. Large tracts are being annually enclosed, which will necessitate an increased production of manure, in addition to a constantly increasing foreign demand.

It is estimated that the production of chemical manure in the United Kingdom amounts to about 500,000 tons annually, and with the exhaustion of the old Peruvian guano from the Chincha Islands, and the uncertain quality of that from the new Guanappe Island, the demand is rapidly increasing, and the rate of consumption points to double the quantity being required during the next ten years.

The amount to be paid to the vendors for the estates, leases and buildings, plant, machinery, and the valuable contents of the factories, goodwill, &c., is £[illegible].

The careful investigation made by the Directors, the majority of whom are practically acquainted with the details of this business, enables them confidently to anticipate a minimum dividend of 10 per cent., after setting aside sufficient sums to meet depreciation and reserve. Mr. Lawes' net profits for the last twelve months on his manufactured and purchased manures and on other articles in the trade exceed £63,000.

The agricultural world has for many years been largely indebted to Mr. Lawes for his practical and scientific researches in agricultural chemistry, and he stands unrivalled as the first manufacturer of chemical manures, which were introduced by him upwards of 30 years ago, and have been in constantly increasing use ever since with the most successful results.

The Directors have much pleasure in stating that Mr. Lawes has consented to give his assistance gratuitously for a period of two years; and that they have also secured the services of Mr. Chaston, who has had the general management of the whole business for the past fifteen years, and of Mr. Rutherford, who has the management of the Irish department. It is also their intention to make as little alteration as possible with regard to the general management in all departments. This, coupled with the practical experience of Messrs. Vickers, Colchester and Langdale, as Directors, will prove of the greatest value to the Company.

In order to fix the amount of preliminary expenses, they have been arranged at one per cent. on the capital of the Company, to cover advertising, printing, brokerage, stamps, legal and other expenses.

A contract dated the 18th day of May, 1872, made between John Bennet Lawes, of the one part, and John Knowles, Septimus Brown, and Sampson Langdale, of the other part; and another contract, dated the 11th day of May, 1872, and made between the said John Knowles, Septimus Brown, and Sampson Langdale, of the one part, and Charles Tattersall, of the other part, have been entered into, and may, with a copy of the Memorandum and Articles of Association, be seen at the offices of Messrs. Hall and Janion, Solicitors, Essex-street, Manchester.

Forms of application for Shares may be obtained of the Company's Bankers, their Solicitors, and Auditor; and also from the principal Stock and Share Brokers; and all further particulars will be forwarded on application to Mr. R. P. Worrall, the Secretary to the Company.

H. CHAPMAN & CO., IPSWICH, MANUFACTURERS OF SULPHURIC ACID, SUPERPHOSPHATE OF LIME, DISSOLVED BONES, CORN, GRASS, MANGEL, TURNIP, AND OTHER CHEMICAL MANURES.

H. CHAPMAN & CO., IPSWICH, CHEMICAL WORKS.—BRAMFORD. OFFICES.—CORNHILL, IPSWICH.

CLARKE & DUNHAM, 48, MARK LANE, LONDON, E.C.

Lawes Chemical Manure Company's announcement , Mark Lane Express, 20 May 1872,

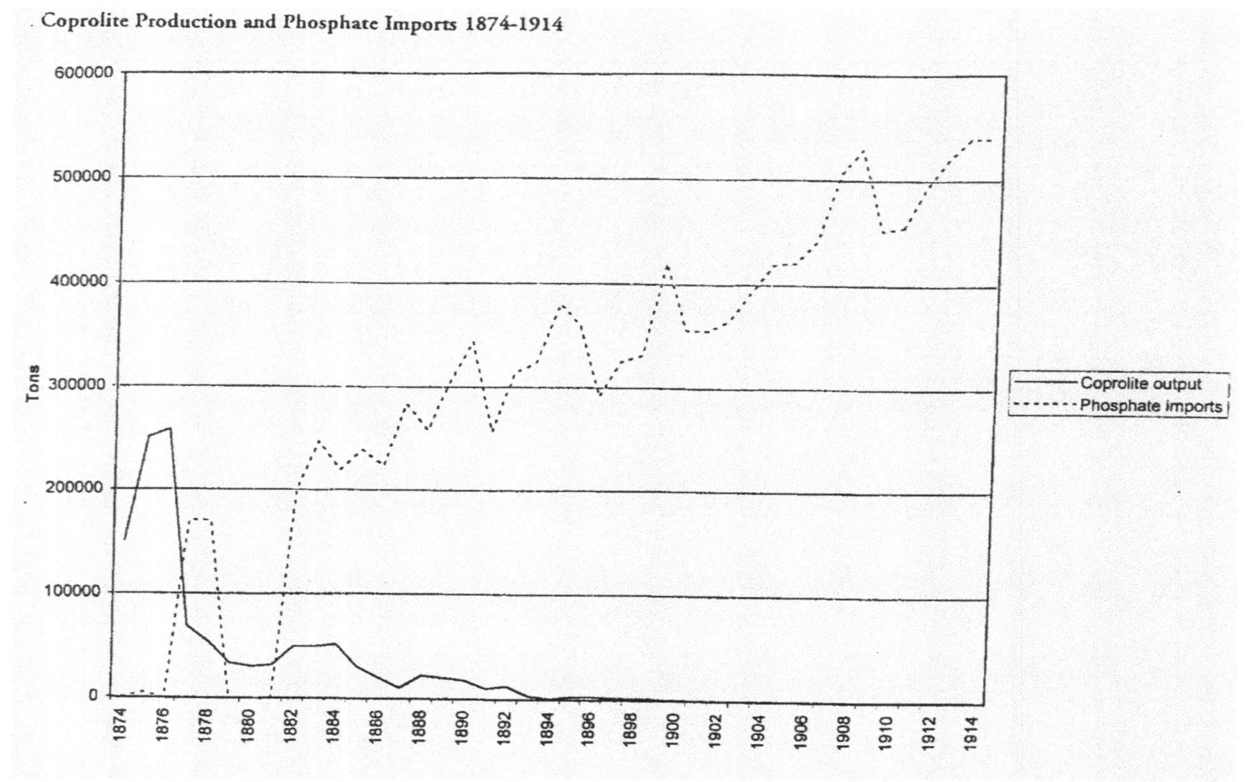
Coprolite Production and Phosphate Imports 1874-1914
Tons
600000
500000
400000
300000
200000
100000
0
1874
1876
1878
1880
1882
1884
1886
1888
1890
1892
1894
1896
1898
1900
1902
1904
1906
1908
1910
1912
1914
Coprolite output
Phosphate imports

*was lying here and there on two portions, the rest remaining unmanured. This last was where the coprolites had been dug two or three years ago, and the other portions undug, needed the manure to bring about an even crop over the whole. It is plain that everyone is well served when a coprolite bed is found and worked; and the discovery of Professor HENSLOW has proved the most fortunate for landlord, tenant, labourer, alike.*

*The whole workings at Shillington are conducted on the piece-work plan. The topsoil is removed and wheeled into ridges and the first 3 feet deep of subsoil is thrown forward-the whole for, perhaps, 4d. a cubic yard. The remainder, thrown forward in great masses, and dug down afterwards to clear away the stratum, costs from 2d. to 3d. per cubic yard, till you reach the layer. This, which is rarely more than 18 inches thick, soon reveals itself by the rattle of the pickaxe among the nodules, and is thrown up on to the surface and loaded into trucks, which are drawn to the washing mill. The thinner the bed the richer generally it is, and a thin bed near the surface is thus a very valuable property, occasionally yielding upwards of 300 tons of coprolites per acre. Worth 50s., or rather more, per ton at the railway station, they are carried thence for grinding, and thereafter for the sulphuric acid treatment to manufactories over the island. And yielding, after skilful manufacture, a superphosphate rich in soluble phosphoric acid, they thus contribute to the current fertility of the whole island from stores of excrementitious matters deposited long ages before the present configuration of the earth's surface existed.* (The Agricultural Gazette, December 23rd 1871, pp.1657-8.)

Readers of such agricultural journals would have been well aware of Lawes' role in High Farming. Even though he had been advertising his fertilisers since the 1840s it was during the boom years of the late-1860s and early 1870s when farmers could more easily afford fertilisers. It was the summer of 1869 when the Norfolk News broadcast the results of his work. Farmers there were expanding their turnip production and the agricultural editor gave them some useful advice.

> "*Mar. Lawes who for many years rendered good services to agriculture by his interesting, reliable and long continued experiments of growing crops and roots with different manures and also a few plots without any dressing whatever, has continued the growth of turnips for a number of seasons on the same ground in order to test the best sort of manure the farmer can apply. It is impossible adequately to state the bearing of the results in a few words... the rapidity of growth and the amount of the crop are greatly increased by the use of superphosphate of lime applied near the seed.*"

(Norfolk News 17th July 1869)

Beef and dairy farmers who relied on root crops as fodder were some of his major customers. The same journal reported six manure manufacturers advertising turnip manures. Guano sales by this time had ceased as the South American deposits had been exhausted. The deposit had been exhausted. This stimulated expansion of the "coprolite" trade especially when the end of the Franco-Prussian War brought a period of peace and prosperity. Farmers were generally better off and could afford the new fertilisers. In fact by 1870 there were over eighty manure factories around the country including eight on the "coprolite" belt. All would have been paying Lawes his royalty of five shillings a ton for their "super".

So great were the profits to be made from manures that there were many cases of adulterations. Lawes' concern at this resulted in an official enquiry by the Royal Agricultural Society who were commended by the agricultural editor of the Norfolk News for

> *"..exposing the frauds that are practised upon farmers by the makers and vendors of artificial manures. The rubbish that is palmed off upon the easy-going husbandman, because it has a nasty smell and because it is cheap is quite beyond belief, did not these checks expose the wholesale nature of the frauds. The analyses of cheap manures shows that many samples sold at 5l. per ton are not worth 2l. and that some are entirely worthless, sometimes not worth the cost of carriage that has been paid upon them. We regret therefore, to see that the Royal Agricultural Society has been cast in 5l. damages and costs brought against the Society by a certain artificial manure manufacturer. The case was somewhat complicated by the transaction taking place through an agent. The question was whether the manure was sold as pure "bones" or "bones and bone refuse." One would imagine there was no great difference in the value and composition of the two manures but the bone refuse evidently means any kind of rubbish that may be mixed with bones. The result should be a caution to farmers to be careful, not only to buy off respectable makers, but to be sure of the particular kind of manure they purchase. Pure bones may grow a good crop of turnips, while bone refuse will probably produce nothing but disappointment."*

(Norfolk News 17th June 1871)

Whilst there were certainly farmers who were able to reduce costs by making their own manures using ground bones and "coprolites" it was not a pleasant task. One farmer, at an agricultural show in East Dereham, told the audience that

> *"...He knew that a root crop was the foundation of good farming. He would not stay to tell them how he burnt his fingers in dissolving bones or how many pig-bellied carboys of sulphuric acid he considered did not pay but the stench was not agreeable, he determined to purchase his superphosphate from a manufacturer. His first ten tons were so satisfactory that the next year he took trouble to carry a pot of this savoury composition to Professor Voelcker for analysis. This cost him 20s. but that was no object to such an enterprising farmer [laughter]. The report was favourable, the analysis was printed on the handbills of the manufacturer as a voucher of quality and he gave an extensive order. The turnip ground was like a garden, the season was most favourable, but alas! by some mysterious process the article which was called genuine, had lost its virtue. His turnips never came to the hoe [laughter]. He dropped 250l. and the bullock account did not look quite so well probably as the return made by the manufacturer of manures [laughter]. This taught him never to deal with advertising quacks, and he has never been victimised since. But it must be allowed that in no article was there so much deception and difficulty, seeing the money's worth as in the purchase of manures."*

(Ibid. 24th June 1871 p12)

## LAWES' BUSINESS TAKEN OVER

There was no evidence to suggest Lawes was involved in such practices. He clearly had his international reputation to maintain. The directors were not able to pay such a large sum immediately. The company director, John Knowles, in his first report to the shareholders, informed them that

> *"Your Directors have paid to Mar. Lawes the amount owing to him for the Goodwill, Property, and Effects purchased from him, and for the Manures and Stock-in-trade taken over by the Company, with the exception of £150,000, which your Directors have much pleasure in stating that Mar. Lawes has agreed to take in the Company's Debentures, bearing interest at 6 per cent., in equal amounts at three, five, and seven years, stipulating, however, that £50,000 shall be redeemed by the 1st of January next; but, as the security is ample, your Directors entertain no doubt about being able to place that amount among their friends."*
>
> (Ibid. Annual Report 1871)

Lawes' name was kept to maintain trade and one of his agents, Mar. Joseph Weston, was given a 50% increase in salary to £300. He was to continue to supervise the coprolite works. (Communication with Alison Taylor, Acting Curator, Hitchin Museum, 31st May 1991) One of the company's first purchases was 800 tons from one of Mr Colchester's works at 70 shillings (£3.35) a ton. 500 tons were purchased from Mr Packard at 52/6 (£2.62) a ton. Lawes stayed on as a consultant for the company but with the financial pressures removed he was able to devote more time to his agricultural research. He clearly had justified Sir E.J. Russell's comment that he had "*laid the foundations of a handsome fortune that enabled him to prosecute the scientific researches which are associated with the name, Rothamsted."* (Russell, Sir E.J. 'Artificial Fertilisers', HMSO. p.90; Victoria County History (VCH). 'Hertfordshire', vol.11, pp.136-7)

By December 1872 a new source of phosphate was offered to the company. Packard offered them 1,000 tons of American river phosphate from Charleston Carolina. They declined in favour of 1,100 tons of poorer quality French coprolites from Packard's operations in Boulogne. By 1873 they had started making purchases of the Charleston phosphates with 1,500 tons at one shillings (£0.05) a sack. (VCM, Lawes Chemical Company Account books)

The Company also maintained his existing coprolite leases and went on to gain new leases in the following areas:-

| | |
|---|---|
| Astwick, Beds. | 1872 |
| Ampthill, Beds. | 1872 |
| Stondon, Beds. | 1872 |
| Cheriton, Kent | 1872 |
| Ashwell, Herts. | 1873 |
| Pirton Grange, Shillington, Beds. | 1873 |
| Barton-Le-Clay, Beds. | 1873 |

(Hitchin Museum, Beaver's diaries; Lawes Manure Co. Private Ledger,1873, p.98)

The early-1870s were a period of increasing awareness of the discrepancies in the labour situation across the country. Considerable unrest amongst agricultural labourers, strikes, lockouts and combinations led to a general increase in wages. Coprolite diggers could earn more than double the agricultural labourers' wages and the increases in labour costs significantly reduced the company's profits. An examination of their coprolite accounts revealed sales in the first 21 months of operation had been £29,789 14s.5d with coprolite wages £23,251 5s.9d. (Lawes Chemical Manure Co. Private ledger I, pp.8,172) This was considered unacceptable and it was agreed to dispose of their coprolite interests. Weston was offered the first refusal but his capital was insufficient on a £300 annual salary.

## LAWES' REVIVED INTEREST IN COPROLITES

An alternative arrangement was agreed. The second annual report of the company explained to the shareholders that

*"Your directors have not been satisfied with the working of the Coprolite business, and looking at the enormous advance in the price of labour, and the difficulty of exercising proper supervision over the works owing to them being situated at a considerable distance from London, and spread out over a large area of the country, they have therefore availed themselves of a favourable opportunity of disposing of it".*

(VHM, Lawes Chemical Manure Co. Annual report 1874)

It did not divulge to shareholders who had purchased the coprolite business! The favourable opportunity was to give it back to Mr Lawes as part-payment of their remaining debt. Maybe some directors were aware that the future of the phosphate trade lay overseas? In their minutes of August 1874 it was reported that,

*"The Lawes Manure Company agrees to sell and John Bennet Lawes agrees to purchase all the Plant, Machinery, Engine, Washing Mills, etc. etc. also the stock of raised Coprolite washed and unwashed and*

*the general business of Coprolite raising carried on in the Counties of Bedfordshire and Hertfordshire under the superintendence of Mar. Joseph Weston for the sum of £2,220 3s.1d. subject to the following conditions. That from 1st July 1874 John Bennet Lawes shall pay all the Royalties and compensation all bills owing to the Company. That he shall undertake all levelling and other expenses incurred or to be incurred by the Company in respect to the Coprolite Works he receiving from the Company the invoice amount of sales of coprolite made between 1st July and 15th August being 543 tons 17 cwt. and amounting to the sum of £1,387 16s.8d."*

(VHM, Lawes Chemical Manure Co. Minute Book I, pp.144 -5)

Having disposed of the coprolite side of the business they invested in new gas works, a tramway, pier and steam cranes at their works to increase production and reduce costs. These additions contributed to the increased profits in 1875. By this time acid production was 400-500 tons a week. Greater purchases were made of the American phosphates and by the spring of 1876 ships were bringing in 2,000 tons a month from Rock River, Carolina. Coprolite purchases started to drop accordingly.

Lawes was one of a number of British companies that had investments in this area and these were to pay off as these phosphates began to flood the British market. Before they completely reduced the demand for coprolites the secretary of Lawes Manure Company submitted in the April 1875 meeting

"*a statement showing the relative values of Charleston phosphate and Cambridgeshire Coprolites and stated*

*that Mar. Lawes was willing to supply the Company any quantity they might require of the latter."*
(Lawes Chemical Manure Co. Minute Book p.188)

The company then signed Lawes' largest coprolite contract for 2,500 tons of Cambridgeshire coprolites. He guaranteed that they would have a phosphate content of 58%. They agreed a price of £3.00 per ton and Lawes was to supply them with 500 tons per month from October 1875 to March 1876. (Ibid., p.194) These must have been from his diggings in Ashwell and Horningsea as there was no evidence of the company purchasing Bedfordshire coprolites until 1881. Lawes' surveyor, George Beaver, reported workings right across the southern half of that county until the early 1890s.

The Manure Manufacturers' Association was established in 1875 with companies like Lawes, Packards, Colchester and Fisons sending representatives to the meetings. It acted rather like a triad to control prices and regulate the industry but it had a difficult job in the late-1870s. Manufacturers were competing by undercutting each other's prices. The Lawes Chemical Manure Company was no exception. It is probable that Lawes was not invited to attend any of the Association's meetings. Maybe, if he had, he might not have been so ken to expand his coprolite interests. (FMA, Minute Books, Peterborough 1875-1880)

At the beginning of 1876 he embarked on another major coprolite operation on Sandy Heath, between Potton and Sandy in Bedfordshire. He had an agreement to work part of the estate of Arthur Peel, MP., and Speaker of the House of Commons. Correspondence from Charles Couchman, Peel's land agent, reveals that Lawes found the time to attend a site visit.

*"In a note received from Mar. Weston this morning*

> *telling me that his report would be in Mar. Lawes' hands on Monday, and that Mar. Lawes will then be ready to attend the appointment, he says, "I have confined my plan and particulars in the present instance to the Coprolites on the south side of the Potton Road for reasons which I explained to you when at Sandy vis a desire to avoid any collision with Mar. Coningsby and his people who are working on the other side of the road." And I have said in reply to it that "I understood your report to Mar. Lawes would embrace the entire area on which the trial holes extended and I would rather not see Mar. Lawes until the whole question can be discussed. And I have asked Mar. Weston to let Mar. Lawes have his entire report at once. It is quite news to me that the "southern" coprolites were to be considered by themselves."*

(Beds.CRO. X344/29/14, January 16th 1876)

Later in 1876 Lawes and Gilbert were taken on as consultants by the Royal Agricultural Society. The ninth Duke of Bedford had allowed them to use part of the lighter sandier soils on his estate at Apsley Guise to investigate the accuracy of Lawes' figures for residual manurial value of different types of animal feeding stuffs. Thus the Woburn Experimental Station was set up. This work was topical because under the provisions of the Agricultural Holdings Act of 1875 tenants could be compensated for improvements they had made to the soil, like the addition of fertilisers, whose efficacy had not been exhausted. As there were reports of "coprolite" diggings on the northern slopes of the Greensand Ridge in nearby Ridgmont and Apsley Guise it is possible Lawes won contracts from landowners there and had the "coprolites" processed in laboratories there. (Town and Country News, 'Aiding British Agriculture', Sep.28th 1934, pp.3-4)

Beaver's diaries reveal that in the late-1870s Lawes was still expanding his coprolite interests in the Bedfordshire area with agreements in the following parishes.

| | |
|---|---|
| Sandy Heath, Potton, Beds. | 1876 |
| Mills Estate, Ashwell, Herts. | 1876 |
| Higham Gobion, Beds. | 1877 |
| Ampthill, Beds. | 1877 |
| Astwick Bury, Beds. | 1878 |
| Henlow Oldfield, Beds. | 1879 |

(Hitchin Museum, Beaver's diaries;)

During the last four years of the1870s there were periods of particularly heavy rains which brought severe floods to many parts of the country. Harvests were very poor and many farmers experienced intense financial difficulties. Many went into arrears and asked for rent reductions. Some went bankrupt and evidence shows that in the worst affected areas many farms went untenanted. The decline in food production encouraged the then Tory government to introduce "Free Trade" which allowed the import of huge quantities of cheap meat and grain into Europe from the North American Prairies and the South American Pampas. The development of refrigerated ships had helped preserve food for much longer. Coupled with four years of heavy rains and poor harvests it brought on what was termed at the time *"the Agricultural Depression"*. Demand for fertilisers dropped dramatically. Farmers weren't buying as they weren't interested in using them.

Although imports of 150,000 tons of phosphates overtook coprolite supplies in 1877 there were problems for those in the manure trade. The Chairman's 1877 report confirmed the depression in the market which he said had *"prevailed for so long a time,"* but there was no sign of pessimism. The following year, although profits had risen again to their peak of £36,629, there were hopes for the future as it was stated:-

> *"Owing to low prices of machinery and building materials the Directors have been enabled to make contracts upon the most favourable terms, and have at a comparatively small cost, carried out the extensions upon the most improved principle. The new plant consists of a high level Jetty, furnished with Hydraulic Cranes, and connected with Tramways with the Works, Ten Horizontal Mills; and all the necessary Apparatus for Mixing; the whole being driven by a compound Horizontal Engine with two Galloway boilers. With these advantages it is confidently expected a considerable saving will be affected in the cost of landing and storing materials, and also in the cost of manufacture."*

(Suff. CRO. HC 434.8728.402d, Annual reports)

The next year, 1879, more imports of rock phosphates flooded into the country and coprolite sales dropped to only 95 tons with prices down to only 49 shillings (£2.45) a ton. Competition was excessive. Profits fell almost 33% and there was hardly a market for "super" with farmers in such dire straits.

## STUPENDOUS AND GIGANTIC DEPOSITS

The availability of far cheaper, more plentiful and higher quality American rock phosphate was not lost on the British manufacturers but what was a potential market winner was threatened by the depression. According to the Charleston

News and Courier the American deposit was of enormous geological interest - on a scale far superseding the British coprolite deposits - and with a wider range of dinosaurs!

> *"These deposits consist of nodules of phosphate of lime, thickly interspersed with the huge bones and teeth of antediluvian mammalian and marine mammoths of stupendous and gigantic proportions; the chrysonicocrisides, ichthyosauri, hadrosauri, stupendous giant baboons, prodigious mammoth gorillas, lizards 33 feet long, and other huge graminovorous and carnivorous quadrupeds; also the squaladons, phocodons, dinotherinons, and members of the ichthaurian, saurian and cetacean families, whales 500 feet long, sharks 200 feet long, briny leviathons, voracious marine vultures and other monster, rapacious denizens of the mighty deep - land and water animals lying in the same bed. These wonderful and awe-inspiring skeleton remains, styled by Professor Agassiz "the greatest cemetery in the world," constitute by far the most valuable fertiliser known to man since the exhaustion of the Peruvian guano deposits; and are an inexhaustible source of wealth to the State and people of South Carolina, and thence to the whole world."*

(Charleston News and Courier, Industrial Issue, 1880)

The optimism was not mirrored in the company's 18979 report. It stated that

> *"The depression which has affected every branch of industry during this past year, has, in consequence of bad crops and low prices, been so severely felt by all connected with Agriculture, that*

*the Government have appointed a Royal Commission to look into the question. It will hardly, therefore, occasion surprise that the sales of the Company's Manures show a falling off as compared with previous years, for not only have Consumers, in consequence of the unfavourable season been compelled to reduce their purchases, but the Directors have in many cases, decreed it prudent to restrict business rather than incur too great risks at the present time."*

(Lawes Chemical Manure Co. Annual Report 1879)

Coprolite prices fell from £3.60 a ton in 1878 to as low as £1.65 in 1881. Mr Lawes must have felt the financial consequences. As well as the problems of increased pumping costs after the heavy rains there were additional labour costs. All the coprolite merchants and contractors experienced financial difficulties and many went bankrupt. Many ceased operations. There were buyouts and mergers. There was such intense competition between manure manufacturers that Lawes Chemical Manure Company dropped its prices for superphosphate from £3.25 in 1880 to £3.00 in 1882 and only £2.50 in 1885. This was less than half their price when they were first put on the market.

The Lawes Chemical Manure Company did not do well. After 10% annual growth over the last three years under Lawes' control the dividends dropped to 7% from 1872 - 1878 and to only 5% from 1878 -1880. Profits fell from £36,629 in 1878 to only £18,821 in 1880. (Ibid.) William Colchester had taken over the chairmanship by this time and the company still owed Lawes a considerable sum. It was he who had the embarrassing task of pleading with Lawes to defer his claim on the company. He argued that

> *"...the great diminution in the profits are well known to you as they do from a succession of bad harvests and from the great increase in the competition caused by the new works which have come into existence of late years."*
>
> (Lawes Chemical Manure Co. Minute Book II, pp.217-222)

As a result the company closed the Deptford works and sold off the plant. It realised only £960. They were compelled to purchase the lease on the Barking works and, despite production of superphosphate at a million tons they had to sell it at cost price or less. There were enormous financial problems and Colchester would not have welcomed Lawes' reply.

> *"I lost a large sum of money, sufficiently large indeed when added to the loss incurred in taking back the coprolite works to obliterate the £50,000 which was paid to me by the Company. I have for the last two years lost money on the Millwall business and in common with other owners of land have suffered considerable loss of income from that source."*
>
> (Ibid. II. pp.233-5)

He went on to admit that his investments in the United States had not produced any income and that his "*pecuniary position"* was not very flourishing . Also, having responsibility for his family, he argued that he was not able to reduce his claim on the company. (Ibid.) . They agreed to pay any remaining debt to his family on his death. The situation in South Carolina was dire. The European depression had reduced demand for river phosphates, The Commissioner for Agriculture explained that

> "... *not only was the market lost, to a great extent,*

*but the prices at which the rock could be sold were very greatly diminished. In consequence of this, river mining became unprofitable. A large number of the smaller companies ceased work entirely, and even the larger ones were compelled very greatly to curtail their operations and to continue with a much reduced force and at great loss.*"

(First Annual Report of the Commissioner for Agriculture of the State of South Carolina, Walker, Evans and Cogswell, Charleston, 1880, pp.11-12)

With this background the early-1880s was a quieter period with the company trying to maintain its market and improve facilities in spite of unfavourable circumstances. The situation in 1881 was still intense, caused by the

*"...disastrous state of the farming interest, to the great difficulties they have in collecting accounts for manure for the last two seasons, and also the very severe competition they also have to contend against many of the other makers offering manures at prices varying from 5/- to 10/- per ton less than the Company's quotation."*

(Company Minute Book, II, p.236)

The census for 1881 showed that Lawes no longer regarded himself as a businessman. Like many other large landowners had done during the 1870s, he had extended his landholdings. Now aged 66, Lawes was living in Rothamsted House and described as "*Farming 539 acres employing 15 labourers*" Also living with him were his wife and grand daughter, a butler, under-butler, coachman, footman, lady's maid and seven female servants. (HCRO.1881 census Harpenden)

Exactly how much the Company still owed him was not stated but some agreement was arranged to their mutual satisfaction. Perhaps it was explained in April 1881 when Colchester admitted having problems with their overseas supplies.

> "*In consequence of Messrs. Wyllie Teacher and Gordon being very much behind in their deliveries of Phosphate under contract he had been compelled to purchase 2,800 tons of coprolite at considerably increased prices and also to purchase 250 tons of superphosphate to enable him to fulfil contracts made last autumn.*"
>
> (Ibid. II, pp.258-9)

Records did not reveal whether these purchases were from Lawes or from any of Colchester's works. Even the managing director maintained coprolite interests throughout his tenancy with purchases from his son's workings in many Cambridgeshire and Suffolk parishes. (O'Connor, B. (1999), 'The Dinosaurs on Bassingbourn Fen', own publication) That year contracts were made for 4,750 tons of coprolites from Beds., Cambs. and Suffolk with prices varying from 72 shillings (£3.60) for finely ground Cambridgeshire coprolites, 45 shillings (£2.25) for clean Suffolk coprolites and 16 shillings (£0.80) for Bedfordshire "*smalls*". Over 1,500 tons of Boulogne coprolites were also purchased at 30 shillings (£1.50) a ton making it the largest single coprolite purchase.

Over the years, through his many publications and speeches on the results of his work at Rothamsted and elsewhere, Lawes' service to agriculture was acknowledged across Europe. He had been given the Legion of Honour by the Emperor of France in 1856, the Gold Medal of the

Imperial Agricultural Society of Russia in 1863, the Royal Medal of the Council of the Royal Society of Great Britain in 1867, the Gold Medal of Merit for Agriculture from the Emperor of Germany in 1881 and the French Cross for Agricultural Merit from the then governor of France. (HCRO. D/ELw.F99) It was 1882, when he was 68, that he and Edward Packard, his Suffolk competitor, were given a baronetcy "*in recognition of his invaluable services in the cause of scientific and practical agriculture.*" (Lawes Chemical Manure Co. Minute Book II, p.338)

This added prestige to the company and successful attempts were made to win contracts overseas in New Zealand, Spain, Portugal, Sweden and Germany. A new coprolite crushing mill was purchased and a new sulphuric acid plant was started which by 1885 was one of the most complete in the country and in fact, it became the major job of the labourers that decade. Records show that the men were paid 22 shillings a week and the boys 10 shillings (£1.10 and £0.50), similar wages paid to Colchester's coprolite diggers. Close scrutiny of all aspects of the company was kept after financial discrepancies in their Scotland office were discovered and inefficient milling practices. Every attempt was made to ensure lower costs to keep a competitive edge. Coprolite purchases continued but not at quite so high levels as 1881 but at lower prices.

As the weather improved the economic difficulties reduced for manure manufacturers, farmers and coprolite contractors. The increased demand for fertilisers renewed the interest in American phosphate. To make up for the loss in trade over the previous few years when some businesses closed down their prices went up. More expense was also incurred to get a finer ground powder from harder Cuacao phosphates. A drought reduced water levels in 1883 causing stoppages at Barking when it was impossible to build up steam to drive the machinery. Yet throughout the first half of the 1880s demand for Bedfordshire coprolites was maintained but at prices which gradually dropped from 30 shillings (£1.50) a ton in 1882 to 21 shillings (£1.05) in 1886 when only 600 tons were purchased. After a slight increase to 1,200 tons in 1887 at only 20 shillings (£1.00) a ton purchases halted. Many pits would have been exhausted by that time or too deep to continue to be economic. (Ibid. 1882-87; O'Connor, B. (1998), 'The Dinosaurs on Sandy Heath', own publication)

Beaver's diaries showed that throughout this period Lawes was still involved in the coprolite business. They show that he took out the following leases: -

| | |
|---|---|
| Chibley Farm, Shillington Beds | 1881 |
| Horningsea, Cambs. | 1883 |
| Barton-le-Clay, Beds. | 1884 |
| Arlesey, Beds. | 1890 |

(Hitchin Museum, Beaver's diaries)

In a valuation of the Company's plant and machinery in 1887 there was a note of £3,883 1s.7d. for Cambridge being "the value of Coprolite Works which the Company gave up to Sir John Bennet Lawes some years ago." Whether this was the plant he bought in 1874 is unclear but it could have been some of Colchester's works. (Ibid. 1887 valuation) A new mill for grinding the imported phosphate was constructed in 1887 and the "chambers" were replaced with six new ones in 1888 to enable an annual production of 20,000 tons.

In 1888, an article in "Modern London" described Lawes Manure Company's barking works and gives us fascinating insight into Victorian attitudes on environmental health.

*"From all parts of the surrounding neighbourhood the position of these works can be accurately determined by the huge chimney stack that towers into the murky air of Barking to a height of 175 feet, and measures something like 28 feet in diameter. This great chimney, it is said, has played the role of general doctor and physician in ordinary to the district, and has done this in a peculiar manner. The manufacture of sulphuric acid is practically the basis of this industry, since the chemical product enters as an important ingredient into most of the preparations of the firm. In the production of this agent a small percentage of the acid fumes generated is allowed to escape by the lofty chimney referred to, and these fumes tend to purify the atmosphere of the neighbourhood from what was formerly a chronic tendency to the development of fevers and ague. The whole sanitary effect of the chimney upon the locality in which it stands appears, indeed, to have been remarkable; and even a case of small-pox was condemned to loneliness and isolation, and speedily died out itself for lack of a congenially infectious atmosphere. Thus the company's works are a distinct local benefit, as well as a source of universal agricultural profit.*

*With regard to the manufacture of sulphuric acid - it is produced from Spanish pyrites, of which 10,000 tons are imported annually, and the yearly output of acid amounts in all to about 23,000 tons. The immense size of the works, of which the sulphuric acid department is only one section, may be best understood from the fact that their structural parts alone - factories, warehouses, sheds and wharves - cover an area of nearly thirty-five acres.*

*The engineering and chemical equipment of the entire works can only be described as the perfection of the plant outfit for such an establishment. The specialities of the house consist in the following: - Lawes' Turnip Manure, Lawes' Dissolved Bones, Lawes' Mangold Manure, Lawes' Cereal Manure, Lawes' Peruvian Guano, Lawes' Potato Manure, Lawes' Concentrated Manure, Lawes' Corn and Grass Manure, and superphosphate of all grades. Each of these is the outcome of Sir John Lawes assiduous researches and investigations into the science of fertilizing by chemical influence, and each article has fulfilled its allotted mission with results that it is superfluous to say have been in the highest degree satisfactory. In the preparation of the above the firm employ their manufacture of sulphuric acid, in conjunction with various products of the earth, viz; mineral phosphates, guano, bones, hoof and horns, dried blood, nitrate of soda, salt, potash, and sulphate of ammonia. The manures themselves are used not only by the principal agriculturalists of the United Kingdom, but large quantities are annually shipped to the colonies, the continent, and America, and the yearly sales now amount to close upon 50,000 tons.*

*The stores at the Barking works are enormous, and, in addition to these, stocks are kept at all railway depots in London, and at Newport, Swansea, Cardiff, Plymouth, Bridport, Weymouth, Bude, Southampton, Yarmouth, Hull, Exmouth, Teignmouth, Gloucester, Grimsby, Gainsboro', Stockton on Tees, Lynn, Cardigan, Saltney, Chester, Penzance, Douglas and Ramsey (Isle of Man), Berwick upon Tweed, Leith, Ardrossan, Grangemouth, Invergordon, Inverness, Glasgow, Aberdeen, Lossiemouth, Jersey and Guernsey, and nearly every railway station and canal wharf in the United Kingdom; also at Belfast, Cork, Dundalk, Derry, Galway, Limerick, Wexford, Westport and Waterford. Agents are established in each of these towns, as also elsewhere; and the head office for Ireland is at 22 Eden Quay, Dublin. The administration of the affairs of this distinguished and influential house is of the most capable and vigorous character; indeed, it could hardly be otherwise in such thoroughly efficient and experienced hands as those of Mar. Elborough, the general manager; Mar. J. Morgan, Secretary; Mar. Wilson, the works superintendent; and Mar. McAllister, the superintendent of the sulphuric acid department. That Sir John B. Lawes has won world-wide fame by the successful operation of the great concern he has founded and developed, goes without saying. That his great services to agriculturalists have been amply recognised and well appreciated is evidenced in his possession of that fame and renown, and is appropriately marked in two other notable and special ways - one his dignity as a baronet conferred upon him in recognition of those services; the other excellent working laboratory at Harpenden Common, near his residence, equipped at a cost of £2,000, and presented to him as a testimonial from many prominent agriculturalists who owed much of their success to the outcome of his labours. In time, if there is today in this country as bona fide and well developed science of agriculture (which hardly anyone will honestly), it is not too much to say that its practical rise, progress present firm establishment, and bright future promise are largely, if not wholly, attributable to this eminent baronet and the notable concern which exists today as a monument to his indefatigable will and energy."*

(Modern London, 1888)

In the same year the Agricultural Gazette published a long description of the works and the editor, Mr Morton, in jocular vein about its noxious processes, commented that the manufacturer

> *"...is, indeed, not allowed to send to waste more than a certain weight of acid to every cubic foot of air; and there stands the ladder and the test-hole, for the use of Mr Inspector, whenever he may choose to look in and take his samples."*
>
> (AG 1888, pp.8-10)

It noted that wages at this time amounted amounting to £24,000 in 1887, a 33% increase over 1880. Perhaps influenced by Lawes philanthropic nature, as shall be seen later, the Company was doing something for its employees. There were

> *"...no fewer than fifty cottages with gardens, provided for some of the men engaged, the greater number having their houses or their lodgings a mile or more away, at Barking. There is a schoolroom here, in which also services are conducted on the Sundays, and where occasional entertainments are given on week-days; there is a general shop, and a public house, a drum-and-pipe band, and a fire-engine; the clergyman pays his visits weekly - even a bishop has been known to conduct the Sunday services - the doctor is at hand:- What more can a well equipped community desire?"*
>
> (Ibid.)

Despite intense competition from cheaper manures throughout the 1880s, profits ranged from £22,000 to £26,000, similar to those in the 1890s but there was a downward trend. More storage sheds were built in 1890 and with severe competition, they bought their local competitor, the London Manure Company and expanded into sheep dips and disinfectants. A fire hit in 1894 which did a lot of damage but a foreign move increased their agencies to include the continent, Argentina, New Zealand and the Cape. (Suff. CRO. HC 438.8728.402d)

In the 1891 census Lawes was described as a *"Chemical Manufacturer"* aged 76. He had several generations living with him at Rothamsted House which necessitated a coachman, two footmen, butler, housekeeper, lady's maid, cook, head laundry maid, under laundry maid, head housemaid, under housemaid, kitchen maid, scullery maid and schoolroom maid. (Herts.C.R.O. 1891 census Rothamsted)

As far as coprolite supplies were concerned, most workings in the country had come to a halt by the early 1890s. The last coprolite purchase of 500 tons was from Potton, Beds. at only 19/6 (£0.97) per ton but by 1894 the Quarries Act had brought coprolite pits under its regulations once they were over 20 feet. The deeper seams being exploited were then considered by contractors as not worth continuing with the additional health and safety costs. The few remaining Suffolk coprolite pits closed at this time.

Foreign “super” from Scandinavia started being sold in the country in the 890s which further reduced demand. There are records of farmers on the coprolite belt getting their labourers to make their own “super” using ground coprolites and sulphuric acid in huge wooden troughs in the farm yard. Long puddling sticks were used and presumably handkerchiefs over their mouths. This was on such a small scale it would only have reduced demand negligibly. In the 1895 report Colchester pointed out that the winter had been both severe and protracted, which could also explain why most coprolite work ceased,

> *"...followed as it was by a period of flood at the time of root sowing, affected very considerably the demand for artificial manures, and this, combined with the ruinously low prices of Agricultural produce of all kinds, which curtailed the purchasing power of the farmer, has had the effect of decreasing sales both at home and Export."*

(Ibid. Annual Report 1895)

Consequently, the prices of all manufactured manures fell, considerably more than any decrease in materials and production costs. Superphosphate was actually imported for the first time in 1894 and as overseas production increased, particularly in Scandinavia, it decreased the company's market and made this aspect of trade unremunerative. This situation continued through 1897

> *"...causing firms who have been doing an export business to endeavour to place their production on the home market, with the result that the competition already very severe, has been intensified to such an extent, that the prices of all kinds of manures have fallen lower during the past year than they have hitherto been."*

(Ibid. Annual Report 1897)

By the end of the century things had got worse. William Colchester died in 1898 and the chairmanship was taken over by T. Perkins of Hitchin. The venture into the brick manufacturing business at that time was a disaster. Poor prices, poor weather and poor prices for bricks in particular, led to the plant being closed and disposed of, leaving profits down at £15,892 by 1900. When the last coprolite pit, according to the records, closed in about 1904, the fertiliser industry had changed dramatically from its boom years in the 1870s.

To help perpetuate his agricultural research in 1889 he eventually set up his Agricultural Trust, which he had promised to do many years earlier. It was not until this time that he was able to realise the remaining debt from the company. To this trust he conveyed the laboratories, the experimental fields and £100,000 for the maintenance of agricultural investigations. (VCH, (1912), 'A History of Hertfordshire', vol.111,p.232) (Rural History Centre, Reading University, Lawes File No.43) It would be interesting to determine how much Lawes spent on his scientific experiments at Rothamsted, what the cost of the field trials and laboratory work were as well as how much he expended on staff wages. Similarly, it would be interesting to see how his financial input into Rothamsted compared to that expended by agricultural societies, Cirencester and Downton, other institutions and individuals. This work may well be the subject of other's research.

Records show that Lawes was still involved in the coprolite industry in Arlesey as late as 1890. His connections with this industry are little known by many who worked and studied at Rothamsted. The enormous financial success of his patent, the subsequent profits from royalties, from his manures as well as from coprolites provided him with a secure bank balance and a high standard of living. His secure financial base was essential in enabling him to practise his scientific farming on a variety of estates as well as a range of philanthropic work. On his death in 1890 the obituaries and subsequent works on this great man paid great attention to his contribution to agriculture. (AG 17th, 24th September, 8th October 1900)

As mentioned earlier he also made an important social contribution. According to Amy Colburn of Harpenden, he was the "Kindly Squire". An article in the Harpenden Parish Magazine showed that it wasn't just Rothamsted that benefited from his philanthropy. Lawes used the wealth generated from his businesses for a variety of charitable purposes.

> *"...Possibly his unassuming friendliness has obscured our sense of greatness, and yesterday's papers showing how the learned public esteemed his work maybe somewhat of a surprise to his neighbours. I must speak of his unselfishness and modesty and absence of vanity, his very appearance and mode of life indicating his character, of his sympathy with the young and all the advance and improvement of the present generation, of his care for the working classes, shown by the establishment of the Allotments' Club long before such philanthropic actions became customary - by the establishment of good schooling for the children of the poor a quarter of a century before the Education Act of 1870, by countless other kindly gifts and words. I cannot tell, but I guess from what I know, the extent of his private charities, given often in secret to help someone in distress or need, given not weakly or indiscriminately, but after due investigation. It may*

*be said almost without exaggeration, that nothing for half a century has been done for the benefit of Harpenden and its inhabitants without the assistance or encouragement of Sir John. For the improvement, even the preservation of the church, the building of the National Schools, the enlargement of the church and churchyard, all were done by him, or his material assistance..."*

(The Harpenden Parish Magazine, October 1900)

Across the coprolite during times of distress there were examples of philanthropic actions - works' teas and dinners, evening entertainment, relief work during periods of unemployment, allotments, coffee houses, religious meeting rooms and reading materials etc. What has not been revealed is the social work that Lawes did in those parishes where he had coprolite interests. Documentation of such has not come to light but it is quite possible that he contributed to the well-being of his employees and their families in a similar manner to those described by Amy Colburn in his role as Squire of Harpenden.

*"At his expressed wish, those Allotment holders who attended his funeral were compensated for loss of earnings by receiving half a crown. Some fifty years earlier he had given land for Allotments - some of the first in the county - near the laboratory and gave prizes for the best kept. For a time the prize was a pig or garden tools. Later prizes were money. He packets of new and expensive seeds in order to encourage the men to grow different kinds of vegetables. A club house*

*was provided for the Allotment holders in the grounds of the laboratory. Charles Dickens visited and wrote an interesting article entitled 'The Poor Man and his Beer'. For a time coffee was provided to replace the beer, but this proved to be unpopular amongst the men. Sir John... started various clubs. There was a Pig Club (in those days most cottagers kept a big pig in their back garden), a Coal Club, a Flour Club (bread was then what was a most important food item) and for a time a Grocery Club (not popular to village shopkeepers). There was also a Death Club and a Bank - all to encourage thrift and self-reliance amongst the working class. Books and magazines were provided at the club house in order that men might better themselves.*

*On the occasion of the marriage of his daughter Sir John arranged for members of the Allotment Club and their wives to go by excursion train to the Crystal Palace. Some had never been on a train or travelled so far from home. Dinner and tea were provided for the party and a small sum of money to spend... The girls who were grass pickers, as part of the Rothamsted Jubilee Celebrations in 1893, new dresses with straw hats trimmed with red ribbons and bunches of poppies and corn with which to attend a garden party at the manor. Back in 1850 land had been given for the first British School - now Park Hall. It is fitting that today in Harpenden a school bears the name of Sir John Lawes. He also gave land for the extension of the Church School. In 1860 when the rebuilding of St Nicholas' Church took place, he gave £1,000 to the*

*fund.*
*On the occasion of his 70th birthday, Sir John entertained old age pensioners of the village to an "excellent dinner of roast beef, plum pudding etc." Invitations were personally delivered, and each guest received a "delicate little bouquet" at the end of the proceedings.*
*On the day of Sir John's funeral some 1,000 people stood waiting to pay their last respects. There would be many who had memories of a man who had given much in the service of his fellow man to the village of his birth."*

(Colburn, Amy (1993), 'A Kind Squire - Sir John Lawes of Rothamsted', The Harpenden Parish Magazine (Link), July pp.10-11)

Hopefully this work will have helped to give further insight into his important role at Rothamsted, not only in the development of agriculture in this country and overseas but also in the changing fortunes of the coprolite industry, as well as in Harpenden and other parishes.

Lawes Artificial Manure Company Annual Profits 1876-1902

| | |
|---|---|
| 1873 | 28,148 0 0 |
| 1874 | 26,328 17 9 |
| 1875 | 31,263 17 10 |
| 1876 | 32,150 17 5 |
| 1877 | 34,887 14 7 |
| 1878 | 36,629 16 9 |
| 1879 | 24,190 17 0 |
| 1880 | 13,821 0 0 |
| 1881 | 22,154 17 6 |

| | |
|---|---|
| 1882 | 26,623 9 5 |
| 1883 | 24,237 16 8 |
| 1884 | 24,937 7 2 |
| 1885 | 25,482 16 8 |
| 1886 | 25,041 0 0 |
| 1887 | 24,953 6 10 |
| 1888 | 23,183 15 5 |
| 1889 | 25,557 3 0 |
| 1890 | 25,887 14 0 |
| 1891 | 23,776 1 4 |
| 1892 | 23,949 9 10 |
| 1893 | 26,362 11 1 |
| 1894 | 22,058 0 0 |
| 1895 | 27,023 1 1 |
| 1896 | 24,958 0 0 |
| 1897 | 22,012 16 6 |
| 1898 | 22,586 0 0 |
| 1899 | 23,006 17 10 |
| 1900 | 15,892 0 0 |
| 1901 | 18,430 0 0 |
| 1902 | 17,441 19 10 |

(Suff. CRO. HC 434.8728. Annual reports 1876 - 1902; VHM, Lawes Chemical Manure Co. Minute Books 1872 - 1875)

www.ingramcontent.com/pod-product-compliance
Ingram Content Group UK Ltd.
Pitfield, Milton Keynes, MK11 3LW, UK
UKHW020239250726
13967UKWH00001B/455

9 781471 697852